OECD Reviews of Risk Management Policies

Good Governance for Critical Infrastructure Resilience

Please cite this publication as:
OECD (2019), *Good Governance for Critical Infrastructure Resilience*, OECD Reviews of Risk Management Policies, OECD Publishing, Paris.
https://doi.org/10.1787/02f0e5a0-en

ISBN 978-92-64-53346-2 (print)
ISBN 978-92-64-41050-3 (pdf)

OECD Reviews of Risk Management Policies
ISSN 1993-4092 (print)
ISSN 1993-4106 (online)

Revised version, July 2019
Details of revisions available at:
http://www.oecd.org/about/publishing/Corrigendum_GoodGovernanceCriticalInfrastructureResilience.pdf

Photo credits: Cover © jamesteohart/Shutterstock.com

Corrigenda to OECD publications may be found on line at: *www.oecd.org/about/publishing/corrigenda.htm*.

Foreword

Natural hazards and malicious attacks against critical infrastructure pose grave risks to societies and economies. Recent shock events – such as the Great East Japan Earthquake, Hurricane Harvey in the United States, the cyber-attacks on the Ukrainian electricity grid or the Genoa bridge collapse in Italy – show how disruptions to critical infrastructure and essential services can result in substantial economic damage as well as loss of life. The interconnectedness of supply chains and technological and financial systems in the global economy increase the exposure and vulnerability of critical infrastructure. When shocks and disruptions occur, their negative impacts can cut cross sectors and borders, and even resonate globally.

At the same time, the global increase in infrastructure investment and the digital transformation of infrastructure services provide opportunities to rethink critical infrastructure resilience. This report takes stock of the changing contexts for boosting resilience across OECD countries, and discusses the policy options and governance models that favour upfront investment in resilience.

Based on a cross-country survey, it analyses the progressive shift of critical infrastructure policies from asset protection to system resilience. Rather than focusing on asset protection alone, a system approach allows governments and infrastructure operators to address asset interdependencies and prioritise resilience measures for critical hubs and nodes whose failure would cause the most damage.

The report also includes a case study on Finland's electricity supply that illustrates how governments can build partnerships with critical infrastructure operators to share information and set objectives, strengthening both trust and resilience.

Finally, a Policy Toolkit for Governance of Critical Infrastructure Resilience identifies important steps in designing an appropriate governance model for today's critical infrastructure resilience challenges. This Toolkit complements the OECD Recommendation on the Governance of Critical Risks, contributes to international discussions in the G20 on quality infrastructure, and supports the implementation of the Sendai Framework for Disaster Risk Reduction.

The Toolkit is designed to support governments' efforts to renew critical infrastructure policies. Going forward, the OECD will work with governments to develop benchmark indicators and conduct case studies to compare progress and improve cross-country learning in this crucial area.

Acknowledgements

This report was prepared under the auspices of the OECD High Level risk Forum by the OECD Public Governance Directorate, led by Marcos Bonturi.

The report presents the results of the work of the OECD High-Level Risk Forum to strengthen the resilience of critical infrastructure through improved governance. This report was co-ordinated and written by Charles Baubion, under the guidance of Jack Radisch and Stéphane Jacobzone. Chapters 1 to 3 build on the Policy Evaluation Framework on the Governance of Critical Infrastructure Resilience, developed by Mary Kate Fisher and Catherine Gamper, as part of a project that the OECD jointly conducted with the Inter-American Development Bank. Ariadna Anisimov conducted the analysis of the OECD cross-country survey on critical infrastructure resilience and provided valuable research assistance throughout the project, especially for the case study on electricity transmission and distribution in Finland. Teresa Maria Deubelli and John Roche contributed to the project with their insights and feedbacks. Raquel Paraqueno prepared the report for publication. The team is very grateful for assistance provided by Elisabeth Huggard throughout the project.

The Secretariat acknowledges contributions from the High-Level Risk Forum delegates who responded to the OECD Survey, and specifically from the following colleagues for their appreciated feedbacks and comments: Ryan Schwartz and Trent Abbott (Canada), Tiphaine Beaussant (France), Kathrin Stolzenburg (Germany), Georgios Giannopoulos and Maciej Kuszynski (European Commission), Christian Fjäder and Mikko Vähä-Sipilä (Finland), Daigo Ota (Japan), Piotr Szufnara (Poland) Stefan Brem (Switzerland), and Elizabeth Lozey and Susan Stevens (United States). Duane Verner (Argonne National Laboratory), Marie-Valentine Florin (International Risk Governance Council), Richard Smith-Bingham (Marsh and McLennan Companies), and Elisa Gastaldi (Siemens) provided complementary perspectives from research and the private sectors.

Comments and feedback received from OECD colleagues Laurent Bernat, Lisa Danielson, Michael Mullan, and Leigh Wolfrom, as well as Nuclear Energy Agency colleague Olvido Guzman, helped integrate complementary perspectives in the analysis.

The report benefited from discussions held at the Workshop on System-Thinking for Critical Infrastructure Resilience and Security, jointly organised by the OECD and the European Commission Joint Research Centre (JRC) in September 2018. Special thanks go to the speakers and experts involved for their valuable insights, and to the JRC for its support in organising this event.

The financial support received from the Finland National Emergency Supply Agency (NESA) was instrumental for conducting the Finland case study and is gratefully acknowledge by the OECD, as is the contribution of the Inter-American Development Bank for the preliminary analysis.

Acronyms and abbreviations

BBK	Germany Federal Office for Civil Protection and Disaster Assistance
BSI	British Standards Institution
CI	Critical Infrastructure
CIP	Critical Infrastructure Protection
CIWIN	Critical Infrastructure Warning Information Network (European Union)
CPNI	Centre for the Protection of National Infrastructure (United Kingdom)
CRISRRAM	Critical Infrastructures and Systems Risk and Resilience Assessment Methodology
DAFNI	Data and Analytics Facility for National Infrastructure (United Kingdom)
DC	Direct Current
DHS	Department of Homeland Security (United States)
DSO	Distribution System Operator
EPCIP	European Programme for Critical Infrastructure Protection
EU	European Union
FEMA	Federal Emergency Management Agency (United States)
FERC	Federal Energy Regulatory Commission (United States)
GDP	Growth Domestic Product
GPS	Global Positioning System
ICT	Information and Communication Technologies
ISAC	Information Sharing and Analysis Center
ISO	International Standards Organisation
IT	Information Technology
JRC	Joint Research Centre (European Commission)
NARUC	National Association of Regulatory Utility Commissioners (United States)
NATS	National Air Traffic Control Service
NCIPP	National Critical Infrastructure Protection Programme (Poland)
NCTV	National Coordinator for Security and Counterterrorism (the Netherlands)
NESA	National Emergency Supply Agency (Finland)
NESO	National Emergency Supply Organisation (Finland)

NIPP	National Infrastructure Protection Plan (United States)
OECD	Organisation for Economic Cooperation and development
OT	Operation technology
PSA	Protective Security Advisor
PSC	Public Safety Canada
RRAP	Regional Resiliency Assessment Program (United States)
SARS	Severe acute respiratory syndrome
TEPCO	Tokyo Electric Power Company
TISN	Trusted Information Sharing Network (Australia)
TSO	Transmission System Operator

Table of contents

Tables

Figures

Boxes

Executive Summary

Critical infrastructures are the backbone of our modern and interconnected economies. The disruption of crucial systems and essential services, such as telecommunications, energy or water supply, transportation or financial systems, can result in substantial economic damage. These systems are highly exposed and vulnerable to a variety of shock events, ranging from climate and geological hazards to industrial accidents, terrorist or cyber-attacks, which can trigger cascading negative impacts locally and even globally.

Given the hyper-connectivity of these core infrastructure assets, compounded by digital transformation, comprehensive public policies are needed to strengthen critical infrastructure resilience. The goal is to limit the risk of disruptions in the essential services and increase the capacity to rebound quickly after a shock. Ensuring the service continuity of critical infrastructures should be an essential part of risk management policies in OECD and partner countries alike, as noted in the OECD Recommendation on the Governance of Critical Risks.

This report looks at the evolving risk landscape and the policy adjustments needed to strengthen critical infrastructure resilience. The analysis suggests that a coherent, system-based approach is best for effectively tackling complexity and interdependency in infrastructure. Partnerships between government and infrastructure operators can also support greater information sharing and resilience investment. A Policy Toolkit for the Governance of Critical Infrastructure Resilience provides concrete guidance for reform, focusing on building resilience up front.

Key findings

Since the mid-2000s, governments have designed and implemented public policies to support the protection of critical infrastructure. Most OECD countries have defined critical infrastructure sectors, established an inventory of assets and put in place regulations, national programmes or incentive mechanisms to strengthen the resilience of critical infrastructure to shock events.

However, these policies, mostly driven by the post 9/11 security agenda, have not always been effective in addressing the challenges of the 21st century's more complex, digitally interconnected environment. Today's critical infrastructure resilience policies have to address diverse and complex shock events, more interdependent systems and countries, and the fast pace of innovation in infrastructure sectors. Ageing infrastructures also present a growing policy challenge.

Infrastructure investments are on the rise globally, offering countries an opportunity to re-evaluate their policies and build resilience up front while bolstering the resilience and protection of existing infrastructure.

A systems-based approach presents clear advantages in designing policies for critical infrastructure. Such policies should address all hazards and threats, ensure co-ordination across multiple sectors (public and private), cover the entire infrastructure lifecycle and foster transboundary co-operation.

Critical infrastructure resilience depends upon governments working with infrastructure operators from the public and private sectors. While operators and governments agree on the need to protect critical assets and maintain service, their views may differ on the level of resilience required, the means to achieve it, and the regulatory requirements that should apply. These decisions have financial implications, and raise questions about who will bear the additional costs of investing in resilience.

Public-private co-operation between governments and operators to encourage dialogue on these issues are useful for jointly setting and implementing critical infrastructure resilience and security policies. Establishing trust, ensuring secure information sharing, developing cost-sharing mechanisms and strengthening international co-operation are among the key challenges to be addressed in creating such partnerships, and require appropriate governance mechanisms.

Governments can choose from a variety of policy tools for strengthening critical infrastructure resilience. The OECD survey identified twenty-two such tools ranging from prescriptive regulatory tools and compensation mechanisms to voluntary frameworks based on partnerships. It is important for governments to find the right balance between mandatory and voluntary frameworks to enhance stakeholder engagement in the process and ensure that investments in resilience are effectively made.

The example of Finland's electricity transmission and distribution system illustrates an effective governance model that fosters investments in infrastructure resilience. Finland has been developing a co-operative framework to strengthen critical infrastructure resilience that stresses public private co-operation, information sharing and consensus building on policy design and objective setting. This governance model has produced impressive results in its first years of implementation. Nevertheless, new challenges have emerged, including addressing the implications in terms of costs for customers, the difference in capacity between larger and smaller operators, digitalisation and climate change.

Towards a more structured approach: seven steps for critical infrastructure resilience policies

This report proposes a Policy Toolkit on Governance of Critical Infrastructure Resilience, which invites governments to address the following seven interrelated governance challenges:

1. **Creating a multi-sector governance structure for critical infrastructure resilience.** Governments should adopt a whole-of-government approach to critical infrastructure resilience, covering the different risks and infrastructure sectors.
2. **Understanding complex interdependencies and vulnerabilities across infrastructure systems to prioritise resilience efforts.** Governments should adopt methodologies and metrics to identify the critical functions, systems and assets that should be prioritised for investment in building resilience.
3. **Establishing trust between government and operators by securing risk-related information sharing.** Governments should establish information-sharing platforms with operators of critical infrastructure for a comprehensive and shared understanding of risks and vulnerabilities, ensuring the security and confidentiality of information shared.

4. **Building partnerships to develop a common vision and agree on achievable resilience objectives.** Governments should establish a continuous dialogue with critical infrastructure operators from the public and the private sectors, taking public expectations as a starting point.

5. **Defining the policy mix to prioritise cost-effective resilience measures across infrastructure lifecycles.** Governments should define a mix of policy tools, informed by cost-benefit analysis, to encourage operators to invest in resilience and achieve resilience objectives.

6. **Ensuring accountability and monitoring implementation of critical infrastructure resilience policies.** Government should monitor implementation and evaluate progress in attaining resilience objectives, with a clear accountability framework for operators.

7. **Addressing the transboundary dimension of infrastructure systems.** Government should co-ordinate national critical infrastructure resilience policies with neighbouring countries and beyond, to address transboundary dependencies.

1. Making of critical infrastructure resilience a policy priority

This chapter provides an overview of the risk and infrastructure landscapes and highlights the opportunity to invest in critical infrastructure resilience. As climate risks and other natural hazards, digital threats, and security risks can disrupt infrastructure services with far-reaching socio-economic consequences, analysis in this chapter expresses the importance of adopting an all-hazards and threats approach to critical infrastructure resilience. In light of the increased interdependencies between infrastructure systems, the rapid pace of innovation transforming infrastructure, and the upscaling of infrastructure investments, the chapter makes the case for adjusting critical infrastructure policies and investing in their resilience.

Multiple hazards and threats can disrupt critical infrastructure

Critical infrastructures constitute the backbone of the functioning of our modern and interconnected societies. The disruption of telecommunication services, water or energy supply, transportation or financing systems can cause significant harm to the well-being of citizens and incur adverse economic effects that resonate beyond the directly affected area.

Major shock events of all types, from natural hazards to industrial accidents, terrorist or cyber-attacks, have demonstrated the vulnerabilities of these critical systems. Their destruction, disruption or interruption could lead to cascading effects across sectors and sometimes across national borders. Thus, ensuring service continuity of critical infrastructures should be an essential part of risk management policies in OECD and partner countries alike.

The OECD Recommendation on the Governance of Critical Risks adopted by OECD Ministers in May 2014 reflects this importance by calling governments to identify where disruptions to critical infrastructure can lead to cascading effects (OECD, 2014[1]). In the OECD Survey on the Governance of Critical Risks conducted in 2016 to monitor the Recommendation's implementation, half of OECD countries indicated critical infrastructure disruption as one of their national critical risks (OECD, 2018[2]).

Natural hazards, industrial accidents, and pandemics can cause severe critical infrastructure disruptions

Critical infrastructure present specific vulnerabilities to shock events, such as natural hazards. Windstorms can make electricity transmission and distribution overhead lines fall down, earthquakes can break water pipes, destroy bridges or tunnels, floods and other water-related disasters can have large impacts on roads, railways, water supply and sanitation facilities, and storm surges and tsunami affect harbours, energy facilities and other infrastructure located in coastal areas . Space weather events such as solar storm can also put electricity grids at risk of a blackout, and endanger satellites and geo positioning systems with potential repercussions on transport and other activities (Krausmann et al., 2016[3]). Industrial accidents may also lead to significant disruptions. Pandemics, such as the SARS in 2009, can overwhelm health systems and impact international air transportation when prevention policies are put in place.

When a critical infrastructure asset or network is affected by a shock event, the disruption of the service provided may quickly lead to large economic or social impacts. Beyond direct disaster damages, service disruptions can have a longer duration, and affect a wider area than the disaster itself. As a result, firms and households can suffer from loss of services, with impact on output, demand and well-being. The continuity of government's activities can also be significantly affected in some cases, including the emergency response, which can further delay post-disaster economic recovery. Examples in box 1 demonstrate how large such impacts can be in a selection of recent disaster events affecting a diversity of sectors.

Climate change, and associated risks of sea level rise, is expected to increase the vulnerability of many critical infrastructure systems located on the seashore and along waterways, notably in the energy and transport sector. The 2017 United Kingdom Climate Change Risk Assessment has analysed the impact of climate change on the energy sector in depth, highlighting the vulnerability of its energy infrastructure to sea level rise (UK Goverment, 2017[4]).

Box 1.1. Impacts of critical infrastructure disruptions in selected disaster events

- The 2011 **Great East Japan Earthquake** and the subsequent tsunami significantly affected the energy sector in Japan. The nuclear meltdown of the Fukushima Daiichi Nuclear Power Plant and the following shutdown of the nuclear power plants throughout the country, led to a 50 % reduction in electricity production, causing substantial energy supply disruptions across the country.
- The 2012 **Superstorm Sandy flooded** key roads and tunnels connecting Brooklyn and Manhattan as well as train and subway lines in in the greater New York-New Jersey metropolitan area. As a result, 5.4 million commuters were stranded without means of transportation, disrupting business continuity more widely than the Hurricane itself. In addition, an estimated 8.5 million households suffered from electricity shortages.
- The closure of European air spaces following **the Eyjafjallajökull volcanic eruption** in Iceland in 2010 led to more than 100 000 flight cancellations and re-routing around the world. As a result, many companies that depend on air cargo to deliver products and key components were unable to supply markets and production systems throughout Europe and beyond.
- The **explosion of hazardous materials in Tianjin harbour** in China in 2015 led to large-scale rerouting of cargos and tankers connecting to the world's 6th largest harbour for weeks.
- The **Chilean earthquake in 2010** caused major disruptions to the transportation and telecommunication systems.
- The **Northeast United States and Canadian Power Outage** in 2003 was caused by trees falling on a high-voltage power line in northern Ohio triggering cascading failures in south-eastern Canada and eight states in the Northeast United States impacting 50 million people in both the United States and in Canada at an estimated cost of USD 6 billion.

Note: Annex 1 presents the impacts of these selected events that led to critical infrastructure disruptions in more details and the lessons learned from them.
Source: Annex 1

These disruptions can lead to significant economic damages and losses

Estimating the economic and social impact of critical infrastructure disruption proves to be difficult to assess. These indirect impacts of disaster events are not as straightforward to measure or model than direct damages, for which classic techniques are increasingly in place across OECD countries (OECD, 2018[5]). Nevertheless, in large disasters the economic impact of these disruptions is generally too large to ignore (Rose et al., 2012[6]).

The OECD analysis on the risk of flood from the Seine river in Paris metropolitan area provides an idea of the extent of economic losses related to critical infrastructure. Based on flood scenarios of different magnitudes centred around a 100-year return period event, potential damages to critical infrastructure such as transport, energy or water assets and networks represent between 35% and 55% of the total direct damages caused by flood. More importantly, business losses caused by disruptions of the electricity and transportation sectors in Paris metropolitan areas can reach up to 85% of the total business losses modelled for the entire area (OECD, 2014[7]).

Critical infrastructure can be targets for malicious attacks from terrorism to digital security threats

Malicious actors have also identified critical infrastructure as potential targets in light of the major impact that their disruption can generate. This holds true for acts of terrorism, and increasingly for digital threats. The emerging risk of hybrid threats, characterised by malicious actors playing with the vulnerabilities of civilian activities such as essential lifelines to impact societal trust in open and democratic societies, have also received an increased attention from risk managers in OECD countries (OECD, 2018[8]).

As presented in Box 1.2, digital threats can affect critical infrastructure in different ways from software to hardware, and through impact on demand. The rapid evolution of technologies and increasing digitalisation of many critical infrastructure processes call for a constant watch of digital security threats and a regular assessment of emerging capabilities of malicious actors.

Regarding the risk of terrorism, transport infrastructures – from air traffic over maritime transport to railways and subways - are highly vulnerable targets for terrorist attacks that can be complex to protect. If attacked, the negative impacts can cascade much beyond the loss of lives, as systems may be disrupted for weeks to follow and repercussions on citizen's trust be hard to regain. Chemical plants and nuclear reactors can also be targeted by terrorist attacks, resulting in large-scale spills that can render areas inhabitable for long time-periods. Terrorist may also target water systems with bacteriological or chemical contamination.

For both risk to digital security and terrorism, insider threats is an important issue for critical infrastructure operators. Having access to facilities and knowledge of security measures provide indeed a significant advantage for malicious actors willing to commit such acts.

Towards an all-hazards and threats approach to critical infrastructure risks

In this dynamic risk landscape, the portfolio of risks that policy-makers will need to address to build a more resilient nation is constantly evolving. Vulnerabilities of critical infrastructure to this range of hazards and threats call for increased attention to critical infrastructure security and resilience. Disaster risks, compounded by climate change, present a set of challenges for infrastructure resilience. In addition, the rise of hybrid threats and associated digital security risks calls for increased resilience of critical infrastructures to digital security incidents. Security measures against terrorism risk need to include infrastructure resilience as well. This diversity of hazards facing critical infrastructure, calls for an all-hazards and threats approach to critical infrastructure resilience.

Box 1.2. Digital threats to critical infrastructure

Digital threats can affect critical infrastructure in different ways:

Malware affecting command and control systems: The Stuxnet malware discovered in 2010 demonstrated for instance the vulnerabilities of the command and control systems governing complex industrial processes such as the functioning of power plants or water and oil distribution networks. Taking direct control of complex industrial and technical processes linked to critical infrastructure requires robust technical capacities. The 2015 attack on the Ukrainian electricity grid was a warning signal highlighting the sophistication of attacks and the availability of tools to take partial control and disrupt power supply.

Ransomware affecting a large set of computers can similarly block systems and affect critical infrastructure operators in their routine activities with potential implication on their operations. In 2017, Wannacry and NotPetya ransomwares led to severe disruptions on a series of critical infrastructure systems over Europe, including the United Kingdom National Health Service, the telecommunication company Telefonica in Spain, the German railway company Deutsche Bahn, or the Danish shipping company Maersk.

Distributed control on Internet of Things devices affecting demand: Increasing concerns relate to the vulnerabilities of Internet of Things devices, which usually have low levels of protection against digital threats. Controlling a large number of devices can be utilised to create a demand shock on utility's services. For instance, the simultaneous switch on of devices can generate an electricity demand peak disturbing the balance between electricity production and consumption, with repercussions on the network's stability.

Backdoors on hardware components of critical infrastructure: Beyond software, digital threats may also come from hardware components. Supply chains of critical industries have become a major area of consideration for policy makers, for instance with the on-going deployment of 5G technologies. In the context of hybrid threats, the intentional threat that information technology suppliers could build hardware and software backdoors in IT/OT systems used for critical infrastructure operations is a growing concern.

Source: Presentations and discussions at the OECD Workshop on System-thinking for critical Infrastructure resilience and Security, (2018), available at http://oe.cd/critinf

A new landscape for investing in critical infrastructure resilience

Aside from the evolution of the risk factors, the infrastructure sector itself is undergoing significant changes and evolutions, which can affect resilience. First, interconnectedness and interdependencies between infrastructure systems and between countries have significantly increased with globalisation, upscaling the potential for shock events to cascade.

Second, innovation and technology advancements give emergence to new forms and types of infrastructure systems, from smart cities to autonomous vehicles. These new kinds of 'smart infrastructure' principally use innovations aimed at reducing costs and increasing efficiency, which may have implications on risk and resilience that still need to be understood properly. In parallel to emerging new infrastructure, ageing infrastructure creates vulnerabilities in many OECD countries.

Third, investments in infrastructure are on the rise globally, which creates a key opportunity to strengthen resilience from the start, provided these investments integrate resilience in their design.

Interconnectedness and interdependencies of infrastructure assets and systems are on the rise

Global investments in infrastructure, along with the deployment of global value chains, as well as the rise of information and communication technologies, have increased interconnectedness and interdependencies between sectors and countries around the world. Increased flows of data, goods, people and energy feed global value chains and sustain economic growth. Critical infrastructures are the hubs, nodes and networks of an increasingly complex web of interdependencies and interconnectedness, through which threat agents can navigate and the impact of disruptions can cascade. Therefore, the failure or disruption of one critical infrastructure system can have far-reaching consequences, in other sectors, or in other locations, sometimes globally (OECD, 2011[9]).

Figure 1.1. Utility and network interdependencies

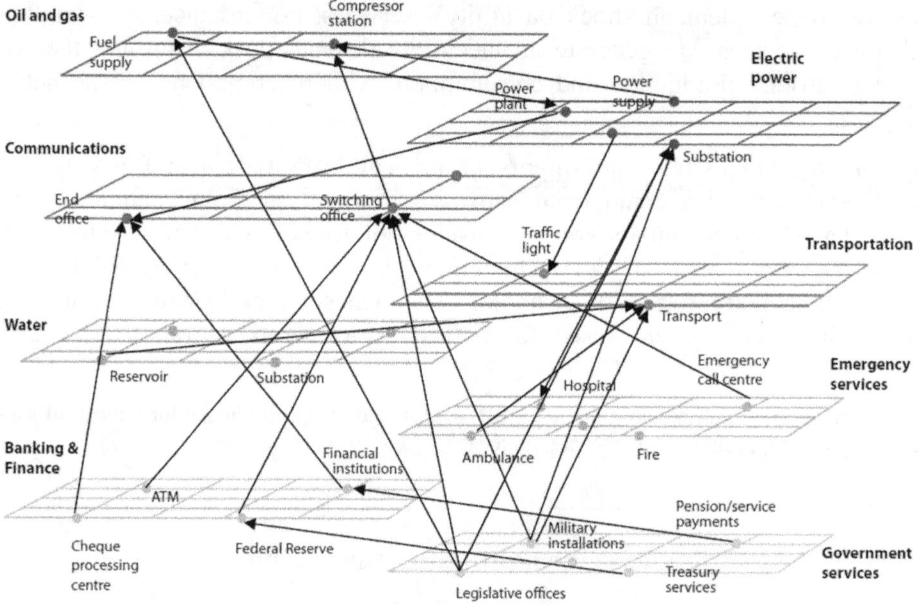

Source: NARUC (The National Association of Regulatory Utility Commissioners), (2005), Technical Assistance Brief on Critical Infrastructure Protection "Utility and Network Interdependencies: What State Regulators Need to Know", US, available at www.naruc.org/Publications/CIP_Interdependencies_2.pdf

For instance, the 2011 large-scale floods in Bangkok affected the car industry of Japan significantly, as suppliers located in the flooded area were disrupted. Cross-border infrastructures such as high-voltage electricity grids are another way through which disruptions can propagate. Failures of electricity or telecommunication systems can have consequences for other critical sectors that depend on power supply or on telecommunication systems to operate, from water treatment, to critical industries or government systems (Figure 1.1).

Some sectors are almost entirely dependent on key critical infrastructure to operate: for instance the aviation sector depends upon the Global Positioning System (GPS) for the management of planes routes around the world; global data exchanges rely on a limited number of submarine cables through which more than 90% of the world's data traffic passes (Figure 1.2).

Figure 1.2. Global map of the submarine cable system

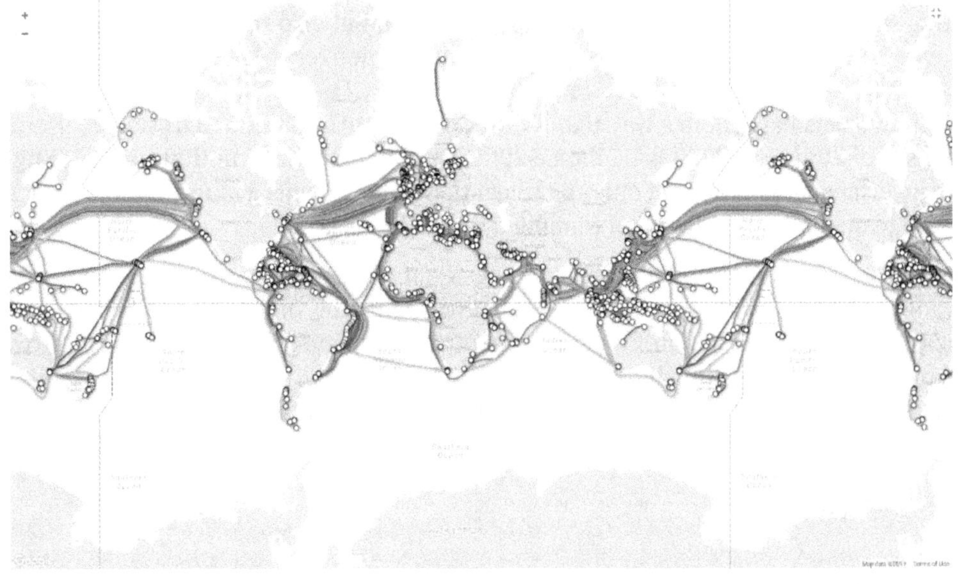

Source: Global Bandwidth Research Service, (2017), TeleGeography's free interactive Submarine Cable Map, available at https://www.telegeography.com/telecom-resources/submarine-cable-map/index.html

Innovation and digitalisation are transforming infrastructure

Innovation is transforming infrastructure systems at a rapid pace, with consequences on risks and vulnerabilities that critical infrastructure resilience and security policies should integrate. From the energy to the information or transportation sectors, large transformations are under way. The energy sector provides opportunities for significant innovations with the increasing share of renewable resources, the development of smart grids, and more decentralised and localised approaches to energy production and consumption. The rapid development of autonomous vehicles along with progress in artificial intelligence promises to change radically the transportation sector. Information and communication technologies have significantly transformed the way we exchange data and communicate in our daily lives. Smart cities, governed by a data-centred approach, aim to combine the data revolution with innovative and interconnected city services, reshaping metropolitan areas, where a majority of the global population lives.

As the pace of innovation continues to accelerate, this has implications for risk management. Overall, the current innovation trends suggest that more decentralised systems and autonomous mechanisms will progressively replace centralised networks with command and control automation. Such characteristics could strengthen resilience through increased redundancy and flexibility. However, it could also produce new forms of vulnerabilities: the multiplication of weak points in decentralised systems and the widespread risk of more damaging cyber-attacks to these systems, which increasingly rely on data flows and coding.

Rising investments in infrastructure provide opportunities for resilience

Major investments in new infrastructures are planned for the next decades and this constitutes a valuable opportunity to ensure that resilience is integrated from the outset. A recent OECD analysis suggests that USD 95 trillion is needed to cover infrastructure investments needs for the 2016-2030 period (OECD, 2017[10]). In many OECD countries, ageing infrastructure requires investments and innovation provides opportunities to make these investments contribute to increased productivity.

Getting such infrastructure investments not only right, but also resilient requires revisiting the overarching governance models for infrastructure delivery. The OECD has developed a framework for better infrastructure governance (OECD, 2017[11]) which aims to make the right projects happen, in a way that is cost effective, affordable and trusted by users and citizens. This framework stresses the need to integrate resilience upfront in the design of these investments, in order not only to protect these investments against hazards or threats, but also to maintain their function running at times of disasters.

Climate change will require also designing resilient infrastructure, adapting or retrofitting existing ones and building protective infrastructure, some of them being considered as critical. The OECD work on climate resilient infrastructure (OECD, 2018[12]) provides guidance on how to ensure climate resilience, through specific designs, strengthening the enabling environment for climate resilience and mobilising public and private investments.

References

Acton, J. and M. Hibbs (2012), *Why Fukishima was preventable?*, http://www.CarnegieEndowment.org/pubs. (accessed on 25 February 2019). [24]

Alexander, D. (2013), "Volcanic ash in the atmosphere and risks for civil aviation: A study in European crisis management", *International Journal of Disaster Risk Science*, Vol. 4/1, pp. 9-19, http://dx.doi.org/10.1007/s13753-013-0003-0. [31]

Bach, C. et al. (2013), "Adding value to critical infrastructure research and disaster risk management: the resilience concept", *http://journals.openedition.org/sapiens* 6.1, https://journals.openedition.org/sapiens/1626 (accessed on 25 February 2019). [25]

Critical Five (2014), *Forging a Common Understanding for Critical Infrastructure Shared Narrative*, https://www.dhs.gov/sites/default/files/publications/critical-five-shared-narrative-critical-infrastructure-2014-508.pdf (accessed on 25 February 2019). [34]

Eurocontrol (2010), *Ash-cloud of April and May 2010: Impact on Air Traffic*, https://www.eurocontrol.int/sites/default/files/content/documents/official-documents/facts-and-figures/statfor/ash-impact-air-traffic-2010.pdf (accessed on 25 February 2019). [29]

FEMA (2013), *Hurricane Sandy FEMA After-Action Report*, https://www.fema.gov/media-library-data/20130726-1923-25045-7442/sandy_fema_aar.pdf (accessed on 25 February 2019). [22]

Fermandois, A. (2011), *Chile and its earthquake-Preparedness, response and lessons*, http://dels.nas.edu/resources/static-assets/materials-based-on-reports/presentations/AmbassadorFermandois.pdf (accessed on 25 February 2019). [27]

Flynn, S. (2015), *Bolstering Critical Infrastructure Resilience After Superstorm Sandy: Lessons for New York and the Nation*, Northeastern University, Boston, Massachusetts, http://dx.doi.org/10.17760/D20241717. [19]

Fu, G., J. Wang and M. Yan (2016), "Anatomy of Tianjin Port fire and explosion: Process and causes", *Process Safety Progress*, Vol. 35/3, pp. 216-220, http://dx.doi.org/10.1002/prs.11837. [16]

Gordon, W., A. Fairhall and A. Landman (2017), "Threats to Information Security — Public Health Implications", *New England Journal of Medicine*, Vol. 377/8, pp. 707-709, http://dx.doi.org/10.1056/NEJMp1707212. [15]

Huang, P. and J. Zhang (2015), "Facts related to August 12, 2015 explosion accident in Tianjin, China", *Process Safety Progress*, Vol. 34/4, pp. 313-314, http://dx.doi.org/10.1002/prs.11789. [17]

Hurricane Sandy Rebuilding Task Force (2013), *HURRICANE SANDY REBUILDING STRATEGY Stronger Communities, A Resilient Region*, US Department of Housing and Urban Development, https://archives.hud.gov/news/2013/HSRebuildingStrategy.pdf (accessed on 25 February 2019). [21]

IATA (2010), *IATA Economic Briefing Chart 1: The spread and shift of the plume*, http://www.iata.org/economics (accessed on 25 February 2019). [30]

Krausmann, E. et al. (2016), *Space weather and critical infrastructures : findings and outlook.*, European Commission Joint Research Centre, https://ec.europa.eu/jrc/en/publication/eur-scientific-and-technical-research-reports/space-weather-critical-infrastructures-findings-and-outlook (accessed on 25 February 2019). [3]

Mattei, T. (2017), "Privacy, Confidentiality, and Security of Health Care Information: Lessons from the Recent WannaCry Cyberattack", *World Neurosurgery*, Vol. 104, pp. 972-974, http://dx.doi.org/10.1016/j.wneu.2017.06.104. [13]

Mazzocchi, M., F. Hansstein and M. Ragona (2010), *The 2010 Volcanic Ash Cloud and its financial impact on the European airline industry*, CESifo Forum No. 2, https://www.cesifo-group.de/DocDL/forum2-10-focus11.pdf (accessed on 25 February 2019). [28]

McGee, S. et al. (2014), *Risk relationships and cascading effects in critical infrastructures: Implications for the Jyogo framework*, https://www.preventionweb.net/english/hyogo/gar/2015/en/bgdocs/McGee%20et%20al.,%202014.pdf (accessed on 25 February 2019). [23]

Minkel, J. (2008), *The 2003 Northeast Blackout--Five Years Later - Scientific American*, https://www.scientificamerican.com/article/2003-blackout-five-years-later/ (accessed on 25 February 2019). [32]

Muir-Wood, R. (2011), *Designing optimal risk mitigation and risk transfer mechanisms to imrove the management of earthquake Risk in Chile,* OECD Working papers on Finance, Insurance and Private pensions NO. 12, http://www.oecd.org/daf/fin/wp (accessed on 25 February 2019). [26]

O'Dowd, A. (2017), "Major global cyber-attack hits NHS and delays treatment.", *BMJ (Clinical research ed.)*, Vol. 357, p. j2357, http://dx.doi.org/10.1136/bmj.j2357. [14]

OECD (2018), *Assessing Global Progress in the Governance of Critical Risks*, OECD Reviews of Risk Management Policies, OECD Publishing, Paris, https://dx.doi.org/10.1787/9789264309272-en. [2]

OECD (2018), *Assessing the Real Cost of Disasters: The Need for Better Evidence*, OECD Reviews of Risk Management Policies, OECD Publishing, Paris, https://dx.doi.org/10.1787/9789264298798-en. [5]

OECD (2018), "Climate-resilient Infrastructure", *OECD Environment Policy Paper*, No. 14, OECD, Paris, http://www.oecd.org/environment/cc/policy-perspectives-climate-resilient-infrastructure.pdf (accessed on 25 February 2019). [12]

OECD (2018), *Countering Hybrid Threats*, https://www.oecd.org/gov/risk/strategic-crisis-management-helsinki-agenda-2018.pdf (accessed on 25 February 2019). [8]

OECD (2017), *Getting Infrastructure Right: A framework for better governance*, OECD Publishing, Paris, https://dx.doi.org/10.1787/9789264272453-en. [11]

OECD (2017), *Investing in Climate, Investing in Growth*, OECD Publishing, Paris, https://dx.doi.org/10.1787/9789264273528-en. [10]

OECD (2014), *Boosting Resilience through Innovative Risk Governance*, OECD Reviews of Risk Management Policies, OECD Publishing, Paris, https://dx.doi.org/10.1787/9789264209114-en. [20]

OECD (2014), *Recommendation of the Council on the Governance of Critical Risks*, http://www.oecd.org/gov/risk/Critical-Risks-Recommendation.pdf (accessed on 25 February 2019). [1]

OECD (2014), *Seine Basin, Île-de-France, 2014: Resilience to Major Floods*, OECD Reviews of Risk Management Policies, OECD Publishing, Paris, https://dx.doi.org/10.1787/9789264208728-en. [7]

OECD (2011), *Future Global Shocks: Improving Risk Governance*, OECD Reviews of Risk Management Policies, OECD Publishing, Paris, https://dx.doi.org/10.1787/9789264114586-en. [9]

OECD and EU JRC (2018), *System thinking for critical infrastructure resilience and security - OECD/ JRC Workshop - OECD*, http://www.oecd.org/gov/risk/workshop-oecd-jrc-system-thinking-for-critical-infrastructure-resilience-and-security.htm (accessed on 25 February 2019). [41]

Rose, A. et al. (2012), *Total Regional Economic Losses from Water Supply Disruptions to the Los Angeles County Economy*, https://www.laedc.org/reports/WaterSupplyDisruptionStudy_November2012.pdf (accessed on 25 February 2019). [6]

Swiss Re (2016), *Analysis of Tianjin Port Explosion | Swiss Re - Leading Global Reinsurer*, https://www.swissre.com/china/Analysis_of_Tianjin_Port_Explosion.html (accessed on 25 February 2019). [18]

U.S.-Canada Power System Outage Task Force (2004), *Final Report on the August 14, 2003 Blackout in the United States and Canada: Causes and Recommentations*, https://www3.epa.gov/region1/npdes/merrimackstation/pdfs/ar/AR-1165.pdf (accessed on 25 February 2019). [33]

UK Goverment (2017), *UK Climate Change - Risk Assessment 2017*, http://www.gov.uk/ (accessed on 25 February 2019). [4]

Annex 1.A. Lessons learned from past critical infrastructure failures

Wannacry Ransomware Attack 2017

The event and its impacts: The Wannacry ransomware was spread by hackers on the 13th of May 2017 and infected more than 200,000 computers in 150 countries (Mattei, 2017[13])). Wannacry is a malicious software that blocks user access and locks files in the infected systems so that victims are requested to pay a ransom of $300 to $600 in exchange for a decryption key to return the encrypted files. The cyberattack disrupted routine operations and caused chaos in large commercial and government institutions including FedEx, Deutche Bahn, Megafon, Telefonica, or the Russian Central Bank. The National Health Service (NHS) in the UK was worst affected when the cyberattack reached information technology systems in hospitals. As a consequence, hospitals and healthcare facilities had to cancel operations, delay treatments, and declare placement on diversion status across England and Scotland (O'Dowd, 2017[14]). The healthcare system in the UK was crippled and large concerns were raised about threats to the privacy and security of patient data and records.

Lessons Learned: The Wannacry Ransomware cyberattack in 2017 exposed the vulnerabilities and risks to information security systems and cascading effects of interdependent and interconnected systems of critical infrastructure. Information communication technologies are the backbone to many industries and the case highlights the effects of a cyberattack disrupting normal operations of several commercial and government institutions across the globe. In particular, it reveals the need to strengthen security of information systems in healthcare – a sector classified as critical infrastructure in most countries (O'Dowd, 2017[14]). Continuity of business plans should be implemented to ensure continuity for the delivery of treatment and services during disruptions. State-of the art technology can create early-warning systems and ensure privacy and security of patients' data and records (Gordon, Fairhall and Landman, 2017[15]). Cybersecurity and protection of information communication technologies are increasingly at the forefront of critical infrastructure security strategies. It should take into account advancements in technologies and potential new vulnerabilities and risks, as well as the interdependencies of our modern society highly dependent on information systems. The security of healthcare information should be a first-level national security priority.

Tianjin Port Blast, 2015

The event and its impacts: On August 12, 2015, a hazardous material warehouse exploded at Tianjin Port. The site was a hazardous material supervising station and a licensed unit of the Tianjin Municipal Transportation Commission for hazardous material operations at the port. The major commodity in this warehousing business is hazardous and toxic materials and gases. The crisis occurred in a series of events, starting with a fire alarm at 22h50 and calls made to the local fire department (Fu, Wang and Yan, 2016[16]). Fire brigades quickly came but had difficulty to access the site due to multiple high stacks of containers. As the site became hotter, police and firefighters started to initiate evacuations starting around 23h13. Following the fires, two explosions occurred within a few seconds of one another causing the ground to shake equivalent of a 2.2 and 2.9 magnitude earthquake and producing fireballs. The explosions and fires caused 233 persons to be hospitalized, including three critically ill and three severely ill ((Huang and Zhang, 2015[17])). Fatalities reached to 173 and insured losses came up to $2.4 bn. making it the worst industrial disaster in years to happen in China (Swiss Re, 2016[18]). More than 17,000 households had doors and windows destroyed by the explosion and 779 businesses suffered losses. The site of explosion was located near a storage place for imported vehicles for companies Volkswagen, Renault, Land Rover, and others, which led to an estimated thousands of imported new vehicles burned, worth more than $31 million.

Lessons Learned: The Tianjin accident triggered concerns about the production, storage, transportation and use of hazardous chemicals – a sector deemed as critical infrastructure. The case reveals many problems associated with failures of risk control and violations of national or industry standards (Swiss Re, 2016[18]). Firstly, correctly identifying and understanding hazardous chemicals and managing them scientifically has become the high priority in risk management and control. To ensure the security and protection of production, storage and transportation of hazardous chemicals, there needs to be routine safety assessments and inspections on complying with those safety requirements. The case further shows the importance of sharing knowledge about hazardous chemicals including: classification and identifying which industries have hazardous chemicals. Enterprises that have activities involved with hazardous chemicals should be required to identify their own major hazardous sources, and carry out safety evaluations of sources of risk. In addition, neighboring enterprises should be informed and have crisis and evacuation plans in case of accidents nearby.

Hurricane Sandy, United States 2012

The event and its impacts: In late October 2012, Superstorm Sandy struck New Jersey and New York, leaving in its wake roughly $68 billion in damages and major impacts on the energy, transportation, communications, water, and health sectors in the greater New York-New Jersey metropolitan area (Flynn, 2015[19]). An estimated 8.5 million households suffered from electricity shortages and 5.4 million people were affected by the loss of subway services. The damages to transport services alone were estimated at more than USD 10 billion (OECD, 2014[20]). Following landfall, the interdependencies of the highly networked fuel supply and distribution system and the electric power sector along the East Coast of the United States became evident. Unlike previous fuel supply shocks following hurricanes in the United States, this event primarily affected consumers not producers. Some of the hardest hit areas were already at a disadvantage prior to landfall, as their fuel retail outlets were low on fuel, or had completely exhausted their supplies due to a surge in fuel demand as a result of resident preparations for the storm. After Sandy hit, many of the fuel outlets that had supplies were non-functional, because their pumps lacked power due to electrical outages Meanwhile, retail outlets without fuel supply could not be resupplied, because compressor stations lacked the auxiliary power capabilities necessary to maintain interstate pipeline operations. These interdependencies between the fuel sector and, electric power sector, and the potential for related cascading impacts, were unanticipated.

Lessons Learned: Four key areas have been identified as being responsible for the observed critical infrastructure failures (Flynn, 2015[19]). First, stakeholders had little understanding of critical infrastructure interdependencies and the potential for cascading impacts associated with system disruptions (e.g., the linkage between the fuel distribution and retail network and the power sector). Second, building standards have not evolved with the development of more modern engineering designs, tools, and practices that are capable of enhancing the resilience of interdependent systems. Critical elements of the transportation system such as tunnels, bridges, rail lines and stations of the New Jersey/New York metropolitan transit services, which serve as the primary means for moving people and goods within the region, are located in low-lying areas and have in many cases not been built to withstand flooding. Third, current organizational management frameworks and regional governance have not been sufficiently designed to address lifeline sector–fuel, electricity, water, transportation, communications and health–interdependencies. For example, healthcare facility evacuation plans prompted the release of all but those patients with the most serious conditions into a community that ultimately did not have power necessary to run medical devices at home or transportation access for caregivers to reach home-bound patients. Fourth there are not enough economic and/or policy incentives for developing resilience and in many cases, institutional and financial disincentives detract from investments in resilience. For example, many public and private operators opt to accept federal financial disaster assistance rather than rely on their own funds to invest in resilience measures. Insufficient regional coordination and collaboration across the New York and New Jersey Metropolitan Areas in managing risks that disasters pose to regional lifeline infrastructures has been another contributing factor that exacerbated disaster impacts .

In recognition of the magnitude of recovery, the President of the United States created the Hurricane Sandy Rebuilding Task Force charged with "identifying and working to remove obstacles to resilient rebuilding while taking into account existing and future risks and promoting the long-term sustainability of communities and ecosystems in the Sandy-affected region" (Hurricane Sandy Rebuilding Task Force, 2013[21]). In its report, the Task Force noted the storm's particularly devastating impact on the region's energy, communications, transportation, water and wastewater management, and healthcare infrastructure and the significant associated delays in response and recovery efforts and losses in economic activity. Based on lessons learned during the recovery process, the Task Force developed a set of 69 recommendations, nearly half of which included a call to develop resilience in the course of the recovery process. In response to the massive power cut that followed hurricane Sandy in New York and New Jersey the Federal Emergency Management Agency (FEMA) established, at the request of the President, the Energy Restoration Task Force. The Task Force supported a massive private power restoration effort, in which electric utilities executed mutual aid agreements to deploy over 70,000 workers to the affected areas. It enabled air transportation of 229 power-restoration vehicles and 487 personnel to help New York and New Jersey restore power ((FEMA, 2013[22])).

The Great East Japanese Earthquake, 2011

The event and its impact: In 2011 an earthquake off the coast of Japan caused significant damage on land and triggered a series of large tsunami waves that severely impacted the north-eastern coast. Inland flooding due to the tsunamis, in turn, set in motion a major nuclear accident at the Fukushima Daiichi nuclear power plant (McGee et al., 2014[23]). Although the Fukushima Daiichi nuclear power station survived the earthquake relatively unscathed and even initiated emergency shutdown procedures appropriately, the design of the site was not adequate to prevent flooding from a tsunami that significantly exceeded site barrier heights. Grid-based electrical power to the area had been knocked offline as result of the earthquake and when the tsunami breeched the site's walls, the subsequent flooding drowned the facility's back-up diesel power generating units and secondary back-up DC batteries (Acton and Hibbs, 2012[24]). Without power, the plant was unable to provide sufficient cooling to three of its reactors which ultimately suffered a level 7 event full meltdown (on an International Nuclear Event scale of 1-7), in excess of even the 1986 Chernobyl disaster (McGee et al., 2014[23]). An estimated 4.4 million households were affected by reduced power supply provided by TEPCO, the Tokyo Electric Power Company. The Shinkansen high-speed rail was closed during two weeks (OECD, 2014[20]).

Lessons Learned: Post-event analyses revealed that the meltdown was, to some extent, preventable. The incident may have caused fewer impacts had the power plant incorporated the resilience concept into the design. For example, the plant's cooling system was functionally dependent on assured electrical power, and the fire brigade response might have been more timely and reduced the impact if traffic routes were not blocked (Bach et al., 2013[25]). Although the Japanese nuclear industry had the highest nuclear safety standards in the world in terms of seismic risk management, it may have come at the detriment of accounting for a wider range of potential (knock-on) risks. These contributing factors demonstrate the critical role of effective regulators and the need for regular safety reviews that account for and lead to the incorporation of both the dynamic and evolving threat landscape and contemporary best practices (Acton and Hibbs, 2012[24]).

Chile Earthquake 2010

The event and its impact: The 2010 earthquake that occurred on February 27 off the coast of central Chile resulted in USD 30 billion (18 % of GDP) worth of total damages and of that total, USD 20.9 billion (12.7% of GDP) was due to infrastructure damage. The earthquake affected a region comprising 30-40% of national manufacturing capacity. Almost all commercial activity was suspended in this area for a few days and while most industries were able to restart production, some major industries, in particular relating to pulp paper production, wine making and oil refining had no, or significantly reduced, commercial activity for months. The total decline in national economic activity in March 2010 was assessed at 5 %. Economic disruption continued over the next three months, finally returning to pre-disaster levels by July 2010 (Muir-Wood, 2011[26]). The earthquake's impacts could have been far worse if not for deliberate planning in the energy sector and strong building codes designed around seismic risk (Fermandois, 2011[27]).

Lessons Learned: Reflecting on the impacts of 2010 earthquake, the Chilean Government took actions to address observed vulnerabilities. At the operational level, the Chilean government committed to resolve the communications outages and monitoring outages that occurred in 2010 with investments in real-time monitoring processes and robust telecommunications systems complete with redundancies (Fermandois, 2011[27]).

Icelandic ash cloud, 2010

The event and its impact: In April 2010, the Icelandic volcano Eyjafjallajokull erupted producing an enormous cloud of ash that progressively moved across the European skies. As a consequence, European air traffic control authorities declared no-fly zones for 20 countries within Europe's airspace due to potentially dangerous conditions of fine ash particles entering into aircraft engines causing equipment failures (Mazzocchi, Hansstein and Ragona, 2010[28]). The British government took the lead in closing airports, on account of information from the London branch of the International Airways Volcano Watch which liaised with the UK's National Air Traffic Control Service (NATS) (Alexander, 2013).

Other countries in northern and central Europe followed the process. The decisions guiding closures were based on approximate data on ash dispersion, but neither data nor maps were provided indicating exact concentration levels across the entire European skies. Closure of Europe's airports and airspace lasted for a period of over seven days with cancellation of up to 100,000 flights affecting 10 million passenger journeys (Eurocontrol, 2010[29]). The airline industry faced high costs of up to $400 million per day (IATA, 2010[30]). Stranded passengers looked for other transport modes, notably trains, the cross-channel Eurostar and ferries which were neither equipped nor flexible for such an increase in demand. If the crisis had continued longer, the lack of integration between different modes within the European transportation system would have resulted in severe problems to move stranded people and commodities, as well as incurred soaring economic losses (Alexander, 2013[31]).

Lessons Learned: The transportation sector which includes aviation and airports is deemed critical infrastructure in most countries. The Icelandic ash cloud crisis revealed the need for increased coordination across scientific communities and channels to exchange information with authorities for better evidence-based decision-making, especially important during crises (Alexander, 2013[31]). The physical thresholds for density of airborne ash for safe flight were defined somewhat arbitrarily and did not take into account that the cloud did not constitute a uniform hazard to aviation. However, the available information guided risk averse decisions to restrict complete access to airspace, and led to increased disruptions of European transportation systems. Furthermore, the lack of pre-existing procedures and planning to manage this kind of crisis resulted in improvised responses to dynamic and changing meteorological conditions (Alexander, 2013). A closer link is needed between operational, regulatory and political bodies to ensure safe, pragmatic and coordinated decisions (Eurocontrol, 2010[29]). The case shows that the management of crises requires strengthened regional and international coordination for response in disruptions to transportation, as well as the need to develop continuity of business and contingency plans to address stranded passengers and economic costs (Mazzocchi, Hansstein and Ragona, 2010[28]).

Northeast United States and Canadian Power Outage, 2003

The event and its impact: On August 14, 2003, a fault due to a high-voltage power line in northern Ohio brushing against overgrown trees led to a system shut down (Minkel, 2008[32]). This occurrence would have normally set off an alarm, but the alarm system failed. As operators attempted to identify the problem, additional lines touched trees and shut down leading to an overburdening of lines that remained operational. Within two hours of the initial problem, the overloaded lines shut down triggering cascading failures in south-eastern Canada and eight states in the Northeast United States. The outage impacted a range of other critical infrastructure sectors including energy, communications, finance, health care, food, water, transportation, safety, government and manufacturing. Ultimately, the blackout impacted 50 million people in both the United States and in Canada at an estimated cost of USD 6 billion (Minkel, 2008[32]).

Lessons Learned: The 2003 blackout serves as a case study of the challenges associated with varying levels of fragmented control, accountability, and authority for critical infrastructure (U.S.-Canada Power System Outage Task Force, 2004[33]). The official bilateral government report examining the 2003 Northeast Power outage described direct causes and contributing factors of the incident, including: "failure to maintain adequate reactive power support; failure to ensure operation within secure limits; inadequate vegetation management; inadequate operator training; failure to identify emergency conditions and communicate that status to neighbouring systems; and inadequate regional-scale visibility over the bulk power system". The latter resulted in situations where for example in the city of Ottawa the bridges that crossed over to Quebec were half lit because the power was still on in Gatineau, Quebec but there seemed to be no ability to send that power to the side of the province of Ontario. These findings translated to several notable lessons learned in the form of recommendations. For example, the Task Force asserted that regulators, the electric power industry, and related stakeholders should adhere to high reliability standards, using market mechanisms when and where possible, but always choosing high reliability over commercial objectives should conflicts between the two arise. The report went on to emphasize that both regulators and consumers should recognize that reliability requires investment and operational expenditures that businesses will be unwilling to commit to if the costs are not accompanied by assurances from regulators regarding recoverability. Prompted by the analysis of the blackout incident, the United States Congress passed the Energy Policy Act of 2005, which enabled the Federal Energy Regulatory Commission (FERC) to enforce new North American Electricity Reliability Corporation standards; five years following the incident, FERC had far approved 96 new reliability standards (Minkel, 2008[32]).

2. Governance challenges for critical infrastructure resilience

This chapter reflects upon the changing context for critical infrastructure policies and presents a series of governance challenges for policy design and implementation in this area. Addressing the increased interdependencies and complexity of critical infrastructure requires a shift from protection of individual assets to a system' approach to resilience. This chapter proposes a series of building blocks to adopt such system's approach and discusses the roles of governments and infrastructure stakeholders in critical infrastructure resilience. It concludes by highlighting governance challenges that policy-makers need to overcome to adjust critical infrastructure policies to the dynamic risk landscape of our time.

From critical infrastructure protection to resilience

Rising uncertainties require more adaptive critical infrastructure policies

Governments have dedicated specific attention to the importance of, and vulnerabilities associated with, critical infrastructure for decades. Until the mid-2000s, most critical infrastructure policies and activities centred on the protection of assets. A new approach appeared necessary given the rising costs of disasters, large-scale terrorist attacks such as the 9/11 attacks in 2001 in the United States, the 2005 London bombings, and increasingly frequent cyber-attacks targeting critical infrastructures. Governments began to shift the focus from critical infrastructure protection to critical infrastructure resilience in order to adjust these policies to this changing risk landscape (Critical Five, 2014[34]).

The resilience focus does not preclude protection, or security considerations. It rather broadens the lens of critical infrastructure frameworks by integrating concepts such as adaptability, flexibility and robustness (Flynn, 2008[35]) (Barami, 2013[36]). Under the critical infrastructure protection paradigm, stakeholders viewed critical infrastructure risk management from a predominately asset-based perspective with a focus on security and physical measures to prevent critical infrastructure disruptions altogether.

The shift towards a resilience-based perspective is prompted by the considerable degree of uncertainty about the intensity and the complexity of future disasters and their potential impacts on infrastructure. For instance, uncertainties around climate change have to be factored in, when long-term infrastructure investments are planned and when measures associated with the continuity of their services are designed. The nature of the uncertainties surrounding disaster events requires incremental approaches that prepare assets and systems with capacities to be restored and rehabilitated swiftly.

Defining critical infrastructure resilience

Resilience can be defined as the capacity of critical infrastructure to absorb a disturbance, recover from disruptions and adapt to changing conditions, while still retaining essentially the same function as prior to the disruptive shock (OECD, 2014[20]); (Chang et al., 2014[37]). This definition includes the indispensable ability to withstand shocks without loss of functionality, limiting the duration of service interruption as well as minimising the recovery time.

Thus, when a shock occurs, on can measure resilience objectives for critical infrastructure on two dimensions: limiting the extent of the damages, and limiting the duration of the service interruption caused by the damages. It is important to note that recovery does not necessarily mean resuming to exactly the prior state before the shock, but may involve changing, adapting to new conditions and improving systems' functionality overtime.

In this context, ensuring the resilience of critical infrastructures is done by ensuring the combination of several key qualities (OECD, 2011[9]):

- *Robustness* describes the ability to keep operating or to remain standing in the face of disaster. This entails designing structures or systems, which are strong enough to sustain a foreseeable shock. It also entails investing in and maintaining elements of critical infrastructure so that they can withstand low probability but high-consequence events.

- *Redundancy* describes the ability to keep operating through a substitute or redundant systems that can be brought to bear should something important break down or stop working.
- *Resourcefulness* describes the ability to manage skilfully a shock event as it unfolds. This includes identifying options, prioritising what should be done both to control damage and to begin mitigating it, and communicating decisions to the people who will implement them. Resourcefulness depends primarily on people, not on technology. Rapid recovery is the capacity to get things back to normal as quickly as possible after a disaster. Contingency and business continuity plans, efficient emergency services, and the means to get the right people and resources to the right places are crucial.
- *Adaptability* describes the means to absorb new lessons that can be drawn from a catastrophe. It involves revising plans, modifying procedures, and introducing new tools and technologies needed to improve robustness, resourcefulness, and recovery capabilities before the next crisis.

International frameworks supporting critical infrastructure resilience

Based on this definition, public policies to enhance the resilience of critical infrastructure should combine measures to incentivise redundancies, system robustness, back-up capacity, rapid recovery and adaptability to new risks or changing risk factors. The OECD Recommendation on the Governance of Critical Risks recognises the importance of achieving critical infrastructure resilience to strengthen risk governance at the national level and reduce knock-on and cascading impacts from disaster events (OECD, 2014[1]). To achieve this goal, the Recommendation calls on governments:

- To identify where disruptions to critical infrastructure and supply chains could lead to knock-on effects across sectoral and geographic borders, and produce cascading effects.
- To develop fiscal and regulatory options that promote reserve capacity, diversification or back-up systems to reduce the risk of breakdowns and prolonged periods of disruption in critical infrastructure systems.
- To coordinate design of critical infrastructure networks (e.g. energy, transportation, telecommunications and information systems) with urban planning and territorial management policies.
- To leverage private sector capabilities in building resilient infrastructure.
- To encourage businesses to take steps to ensure business continuity, with a specific focus on critical infrastructure operators by developing standards and toolkits designed to manage risks to operations or the delivery of core services.
- To ensure that critical infrastructure, information systems and networks still function in the aftermath of a shock.
- To ensure first responders maintain and exercise emergency plans in case of a shock event that disrupts the functioning of critical infrastructure networks.

Following the adoption of the OECD Recommendation on the Governance of Critical Risks in 2014, several international fora gave recognition to the importance of infrastructure resilience. The G7 Ise-Shima Principles for Promoting Quality Infrastructure Investments (G7, 2016[38]) emphasizes resilience against natural hazards, terrorism and cyber-attack risks to ensure reliable operation and economic efficiency in view of life-cycle cost. Similarly, the UN Sendai Framework for Disaster Risk Reduction (United Nations Office for Disaster Risk Reduction, 2015[39]) calls countries to "substantially reduce disaster damage to critical infrastructure and disruption of basic services" and the UN Sustainable Development Goal 9 to build resilient infrastructure. Regarding specifically terrorism, the UN Security council Resolution 2341 recognised the "growing importance of ensuring reliability and resilience of critical infrastructure and its protection from terrorist attacks for national security, public safety and the economy of the concerned States as well as wellbeing and welfare of their population" (United Nations Security Council, 2017[40]). The overarching OECD Framework on the Governance of Infrastructure (OECD, 2017[11]) also highlights infrastructure resilience as one if its 10 key governance challenges.

Adopting a system's approach to critical infrastructure resilience

The shift from critical infrastructure protection to resilience aims to address key changes of the risk landscape, marked by increased uncertainties. In order to better integrate the complexity, interdependencies and interconnectedness of critical infrastructure, adopting a systemic approach to critical infrastructure resilience provides complementary perspectives.

Barami (2013) emphasises the complex and multi-faceted nature of critical infrastructure resilience. Barami applies a risk-based and layered approach accounting for complex infrastructures interdependencies, while considering potential solutions applicable through the infrastructure system lifecycle (i.e., design, construction, and operation). Resilience is therefore defined not as a single outcome or an exclusively post-disaster recovery capability but rather as a dynamic process that applies a risk and lifecycle-based method for addressing the vulnerabilities of critical infrastructure systems, making systems more fault-tolerant, more efficient, smarter, and better able to adapt to unexpected challenges (Barami, 2013[36]).

The OECD High-Level Risk Forum workshop on "System-thinking for Critical Infrastructure resilience" (OECD and EU JRC, 2018[41]), extended this notion of system approach applied to critical infrastructure resilience, and proposed a series of key attributes that public policies should consider in this area:

- *All-hazards and threats*: Single-hazard policies are not sufficient to build infrastructure resilience. The critical infrastructure impacts of Superstorm Sandy in New York, which had engaged in substantial protection activities following 9/11 demonstrated that protective activities alone are not sufficient to address the range of potential critical infrastructure disruptions and associated cascading risks. Adopting an all-hazard and threat approach to critical infrastructure resilience enables policy makers and operators to better prepare for the unexpected.
- *System-level*: Initially, critical infrastructure protection policies focused primarily on setting up protection measures at asset-level. However infrastructure assets are usually only the components of a wider complex system, which should be considered in its entirety in a comprehensive resilience strategy. Some of the system's assets are more critical than others, because of dependencies or (non)-existing redundancies for instance. A system approach allows for prioritising the most critical components, through dependency modelling and criticality assessments, as well as to address weak points that otherwise create critical vulnerabilities for the entire system.

- *Multi sectoral*: Addressing interdependencies requires policy makers and operators to go beyond a system-level approach and to target the critical infrastructure sectors together in a comprehensive resilience policy. While infrastructure operators tend to be well aware of their own dependencies upon critical sectors (e.g.: electricity, payment systems), they may not be as conscious of the dependencies others have upon their own services. From interdependency mapping to developing shared business continuity objectives, a multi-sectoral approach is essential to a comprehensive critical infrastructure resilience policy.
- *Transboundary dimension*: Similarly, interdependencies and interconnectedness cannot be fully understood without incorporating their international dimension. Hazards and threats do not stop at national borders. In some cases, critical infrastructure systems cross borders, providing services in multiple countries. Infrastructure operators can also manage critical infrastructure in several countries. This makes it more compelling to integrate international cooperation in critical infrastructure resilience policies. Sharing good practices, adopting common approaches, developing joint standards in critical infrastructure resilience are among the policy options that can foster international cooperation in this area.
- *Life cycle approach*: Different resilience and security measures can apply to the different phases of the infrastructure life-cycle: integrating robustness and redundancies requires investments in the design phase, while developing business continuity planning pertains more to the operation phase and adaptability can be based on infrastructure retrofitting. Thus, it is important to set-up a comprehensive policy that enables resilience throughout the life cycle of critical infrastructures, with applications from the design phase to its operations and maintenance, and retrofitting.
- *Entire risk management cycle*: A comprehensive resilience policy should incorporate measures throughout the entire disaster risk management cycle, from risk assessment, over risk prevention, emergency preparedness and response, to recovery and reconstruction (Moteff, 2012[42]). Critical infrastructure resilience has specificities in each of these phases. Risk assessment should incorporate dependencies and criticality assessment. Risk prevention includes robustness measures in the design phase as well as dedicated awareness raising dialogues with infrastructure operators. Emergency preparedness and response required tailored warning systems, business continuity measures and back-ups, and dedicated emergency teams and capabilities. The recovery and reconstruction phase should integrate degraded mode, rapid restoration plans as well as dedicated financing schemes, including for building back better.
- *Risk-based and layered approach*: Given the considerable degree of uncertainty about the intensity and the complexity of future disasters, the manifold dimensions of vulnerability of infrastructure systems, and all the interrelationships between these systems, the prioritisation of resilience measures is essential. Only a risk-based and layered approach can account for complex infrastructures interdependencies, while considering potential solutions applicable through the infrastructure systems across the life-cycle (Barami, 2013[36]).

Governance challenges for critical infrastructure resilience policies

The multiple stakeholders for infrastructure resilience

Infrastructure design, investment, construction, ownership, operations or regulation involve multiple stakeholders, which all have a role to play in building resilience. As identified in the OECD Framework for better Governance of Infrastructure (OECD, 2017[11]), there are many ways to provide infrastructure services. The public sector's role can vary and hybrid forms exist. With infrastructure ownership moving from government provision through state-owned enterprises to privatisation in the last decades, government's control over infrastructure assets goes decreasing. Similarly, the mode of infrastructure delivery, from traditional public procurement to concessions or public-private partnerships, will influence how resilience can be integrated in infrastructure design and operations. In this context, risk governance and resilience become intrinsically linked to the broader issue of infrastructure governance and policy-making. With the current trends towards increased global investments in infrastructure, making sure resilience investments are adequately scaled requires that infrastructure governance models make resilience one of the decision-making criteria.

Critical infrastructure owners and operators bear the primary responsibility for protecting their assets and maintaining the continuity of the services they provide. Be they public, private or of a hybrid form, owners would normally want to protect their capital asset against suffering damages or destruction from a disaster, or another shock event. Similarly, operators have a strong interest in maintaining the continuity of their services and avoid disruptions, not only because of the losses they can potentially suffer when services stop, but also because they are concerned with their reputation and image towards their clients or users. Nevertheless, owners and operators cannot address all their vulnerabilities on their own and may not have incentives to assess a complete overview of the full extent of their interdependencies. Interdependencies between critical infrastructure sectors and the potential cascading effects that may follow in case of disaster require cooperation across sectors.

Which role for governments?

Governments have a key role to play in critical infrastructure resilience, as responsible to provide security and safety to citizens, but also as an infrastructure policy-maker, and regulator, owner or operator in some cases, and major user or client. Officials in charge of the governance of critical risks have to coordinate across several functions in government and ensure that, on behalf of the general interest, all relevant policy objectives can be achieved at the same time, balancing the relevant trade-offs. This list highlights the manifold dimensions that governments need to incorporate in the design of their national critical infrastructure security and resilience policy.

First, as stated in the OECD Recommendation on the Governance of Critical Risks, governments have the responsibility to set the preparedness levels at the nation scale, as part of their national strategy for the governance of critical risks. In the new landscape of critical risks that governments are confronted to, setting up national objectives for critical infrastructure security and resilience is fundamental to contribute to the overall resilience of nations. Most OECD countries have now set-up critical infrastructure security and resilience strategies and programmes (see Chapter 3). In light of the interdependencies between the different infrastructure sectors, government has also an important role to play in guaranteeing that these interdependencies are properly disclosed and addressed, as well as to avoid related policy loopholes.

Second, governments have a key role in infrastructure policy-making and oversight. Making sure that infrastructure contributes best to productivity and ensures equal opportunities and equal access to services for citizens are key policy objectives for infrastructure delivery (OECD, 2017[11]). Government's oversight and regulatory function can be delegated to a sectoral regulator, who will have the mandate to set-up key objectives and to regulate the operations in the sector. In this respect, the concern for resilience and the need to ensure sufficient reserve capacity, may have to be balanced with the need to maintain a level playing field and instil competition to drive prices down and improve consumer surplus, while not jeopardizing the acceptable level of risk.

Third, government can be an infrastructure owner and operator, either through direct provision, state owned enterprises, or other modes of infrastructure services. By applying resilience and security standards to the infrastructure systems that it is responsible for, government can lead the way as a role model. This can also be revealing for government on the costs incurred for resilient investments, which can potentially better inform decision-making and related cost-benefit analyses for critical infrastructure resilience investments.

Finally, governments are also infrastructure users or clients, and therefore depend upon various critical infrastructure to maintain their own continuity. As such, governments have specific expectations for the continuity of critical infrastructure underpinning government's key functions. Some countries for instance have designated government as one of the critical infrastructures sectors in their policy. A question for governments in the design of their critical infrastructure policy is whether its own continuity would request some specific resilience levels and/ or standards for critical infrastructure resilience compared to other sectors.

Partnering for critical infrastructure resilience and related governance challenges

Although governments continue to own, invest in, operate and regulate critical infrastructure in some sectors, an increasing share of critical infrastructure is either privately owned or operated. In some countries, the private sector operates most of these infrastructure systems. Therefore, the resilience of these systems depends upon governments partnering with infrastructure operators from the public and private sectors in resilience efforts through the establishment of relevant governance arrangements.

Critical infrastructure operators and governments often agree on the need to protect key assets and maintain their services, but views can differ on the level of security resilience required, the means to achieve it, and the requirements that should apply. Policy issues to be addressed include the criticality of specific installations to the broader network, maintenance of a level playing field between operators, the acceptable duration of 'down time', the distribution of costs to different stakeholders in paying for resilience and circumventing potential situations of free-riding.

Policy approaches that are limited to mandatory measures requiring critical infrastructure operators to put resilience measures in place are not always the most appropriate, as it can, among other issues, become a problem of competition and willingness and ability to pay by the providers. Complementary governance approaches that foster regular exchanges, information sharing, mutual trust, and potentially balanced public financial support for investments in critical infrastructure resilience can potentially lead to better outcomes when carefully designed. An effective collaboration between the government and critical infrastructure providers to develop and implement the policy should enable government services to more effectively fulfil their tasks (such as monitoring, early warning, prevention investment or emergency response) but in a way that does not compromise the private sector interests, including confidentiality.

Establishing partnerships between governments and operators (public and private) to encourage dialogue on these issues is a useful approach to jointly build critical infrastructure resilience and security policies, and implement them. In any case, such dialogue will have to provide solutions to overcome the following governance challenges for critical infrastructure security and resilience:

- *Establishing trust* : critical infrastructure operators may not always be willing to share information on their vulnerabilities to hazards and threats with the government, as well as with other operators that depend on them or *vice-versa*
- *Security of information-sharing*: ensuring that information on vulnerability as well as on resilience investments by infrastructure operators remains confidential is a key aspect, especially in competitive sectors.
- *Cost-sharing mechanisms*: another important aspect, from an economic standpoint, will be to know at which "price" resilience can be achieved and who will pay for resilience investments.
- *International cooperation*: in light of the transboundary dimension of critical infrastructure systems, governance mechanisms must include an international dimension.
- *Rapid changes and advancements in technology*: with the rapid pace of innovation in many infrastructure sectors, strengthening their resilience requires adapted solutions, as classic regulations might not be able to keep up with innovations.

References

Barami, B. (2013), *Infrastructure Resiliency: A Risk-Based Framework*, US Department of Transportation, https://www.volpe.dot.gov/sites/volpe.dot.gov/files/docs/Infrastructure%20Resiliency_A%20Risk-Based%20Framework.pdf (accessed on 25 February 2019). [36]

Chang, S. et al. (2014), "Toward Disaster-Resilient Cities: Characterizing Resilience of Infrastructure Systems with Expert Judgments", *Risk Analysis*, Vol. 34/3, pp. 416-434, http://dx.doi.org/10.1111/risa.12133. [37]

Critical Five (2014), *Forging a Common Understanding for Critical Infrastructure Shared Narrative*, https://www.dhs.gov/sites/default/files/publications/critical-five-shared-narrative-critical-infrastructure-2014-508.pdf (accessed on 25 February 2019). [34]

Flynn, S. (2008), "America the Resilient, Defying Terrorism and Mitigating Natural Disasters", *Foreign Affairs*, https://www.foreignaffairs.com/articles/2008-03-02/america-resilient (accessed on 25 February 2019). [35]

G7 (2016), *G7 Ise-Shima Leaders' Declaration*, https://www.mofa.go.jp/files/000160266.pdf (accessed on 25 February 2019). [38]

Moteff, J. (2012), *CRS Report for Congress Critical Infrastructure Resilience: The Evolution of Policy and Programs and Issues for Congress*, Congressional Research Service, https://fas.org/sgp/crs/homesec/R42683.pdf (accessed on 25 February 2019). [42]

OECD (2017), *Getting Infrastructure Right: A framework for better governance*, OECD Publishing, Paris, https://dx.doi.org/10.1787/9789264272453-en. [11]

OECD (2014), *Boosting Resilience through Innovative Risk Governance*, OECD Reviews of Risk Management Policies, OECD Publishing, Paris, https://dx.doi.org/10.1787/9789264209114-en. [20]

OECD (2014), *Recommendation of the Council on the Governance of Critical Risks*, http://www.oecd.org/gov/risk/Critical-Risks-Recommendation.pdf (accessed on 25 February 2019). [1]

OECD (2011), *Future Global Shocks: Improving Risk Governance*, OECD Reviews of Risk Management Policies, OECD Publishing, Paris, https://dx.doi.org/10.1787/9789264114586-en. [9]

OECD and EU JRC (2018), *System thinking for critical infrastructure resilience and security - OECD/ JRC Workshop - OECD*, http://www.oecd.org/gov/risk/workshop-oecd-jrc-system-thinking-for-critical-infrastructure-resilience-and-security.htm (accessed on 25 February 2019). [41]

United Nations Office for Disaster Risk Reduction (2015), *Sendai Framework for Disaster Risk Reduction 2015 - 2030*, https://www.unisdr.org/files/43291_sendaiframeworkfordrren.pdf (accessed on 25 February 2019). [39]

United Nations Security Council (2017), *Security Council Resolution 2341 - Threats to international peace and security caused by terrorist acts*, http://unscr.com/en/resolutions/2341 (accessed on 25 February 2019). [40]

3. State of play in the governance of critical infrastructure resilience

This chapter provides an overview of critical infrastructure resilience policies across OECD countries. Based on a cross-country survey, the chapter takes stock of the various approaches taken by countries to define critical infrastructure, target specific infrastructure sectors and assess their criticality. The chapter also discusses the different forms of partnerships between government and operators and reviews the policy tools used by governments to foster critical infrastructure resilience.

Government critical infrastructure policies in OECD countries

Critical infrastructure strategies and programmes

Comprehensive multi-sectoral public policies to support the resilience or protection of critical infrastructures began to appear in the mid-2000. Out of the 34 OECD countries who responded to the Survey on the Governance of Critical Risks, 90% indicated that they have designated specific infrastructure sectors as critical (OECD, 2018[2]). Many OECD countries have defined critical infrastructure sectors, established an inventory of assets through a criticality and risk assessment process, and set-up national programmes to strengthen their resilience to shocks. Such programmes are usually built on a governance mechanism that allows information sharing between government and critical infrastructure operators and includes a combination of policy tools ranging from regulation to incentive mechanisms to support the implementation of critical infrastructure resilience objectives. A list of these national strategies or programmes is provided in Annex 1.

This section of the report goes into more details of how these national policies are designed and implemented, with the aim to provide a state-of-play across OECD countries. Country's responses to the OECD Survey on Critical Infrastructure, conducted in 2017-2018, helped inform this section (the overall results are presented in Annexes 3.A to 3.D). Twenty-five OECD countries responded to the survey: Austria, Belgium, Canada, Czech Republic, Estonia, Finland, France, Germany, Ireland, Israel, Korea, Latvia, Luxembourg, the Netherlands, New Zealand, Norway, Poland, Portugal, Slovak Republic, Spain, Sweden, Switzerland, Turkey, the United Kingdom and the United States.

Definitions of critical infrastructure vary across countries

Defining critical infrastructure is a necessary first step in setting up a critical infrastructure security and resilience policy. As shown in Annex 3.A, official definitions of critical infrastructure vary across countries. Some definitions refer to critical infrastructure as infrastructure whose functioning is vital or essential to economic and social well-being, while others stress their importance for the functioning of the State or national security.

In half of the 28 definitions gathered from the survey and desk-research, critical infrastructure is described as a combination of both vital processes for societal well-being and a security concern of the state. The other half remain focused on societal well-being and safety only.

Another observation reveals the growing concern around interconnectedness and interdependencies of critical infrastructure and the need to adopt a system's approach. This is found in many definitions that define in detail critical infrastructure as a combination of networks, systems, facilities, and technologies that contribute to delivering essential services or support vital functions. Other definitions also include the institutional or organisational structures supporting service delivery.

Although definitions vary, it may be agreed that an overarching notion of critical infrastructure means that a disruption will have severe consequences on socio-economic well-being and public safety, including national security. Australia, Canada, New Zealand, the United Kingdom, and the United States have developed a shared narrative and definition of critical infrastructure, also known as nationally significant infrastructure: the 'systems, assets, facilities and networks that provide essential services and are necessary for the national security, economic security, prosperity, and health and safety of their respective nations (Critical Five, 2014[34]).

An important aspect is that definition of critical infrastructure should not be static and updating and revising this definition can be a response to a dynamic national and international risk landscape. For instance, Switzerland is currently reviewing and simplifying its definition to “Critical infrastructures are processes, systems and facilities that are essential for the functioning of the economy and the well-being of the population, respectively.” This simplification will allow to adjust the scope of its critical infrastructure programme to changing conditions more easily than before when the definition was more prescriptive. Similarly, in the United Kingdom, the definition has evolved to include impacts on national security, national defence, or the functioning of the state among the criteria to define critical national infrastructure.

What are the critical infrastructure sectors?

The aim of defining critical infrastructure is to target sectors that are most crucial to societal and economic security and stability. Along with the definitions, lists of sectors also vary across countries. A comparative table that maps out sectors deemed critical infrastructure allows to survey general trends and sectors that are more country-specific. The table in Annex 3.C presents a cross-country comparison of how countries differ on categorising critical infrastructure sectors, while Figure 3.1 makes a synthesis of the most commonly types of critical infrastructure sectors across OECD countries from the OECD survey.

Figure 3.1. Sectors of designated critical infrastructure across OECD countries

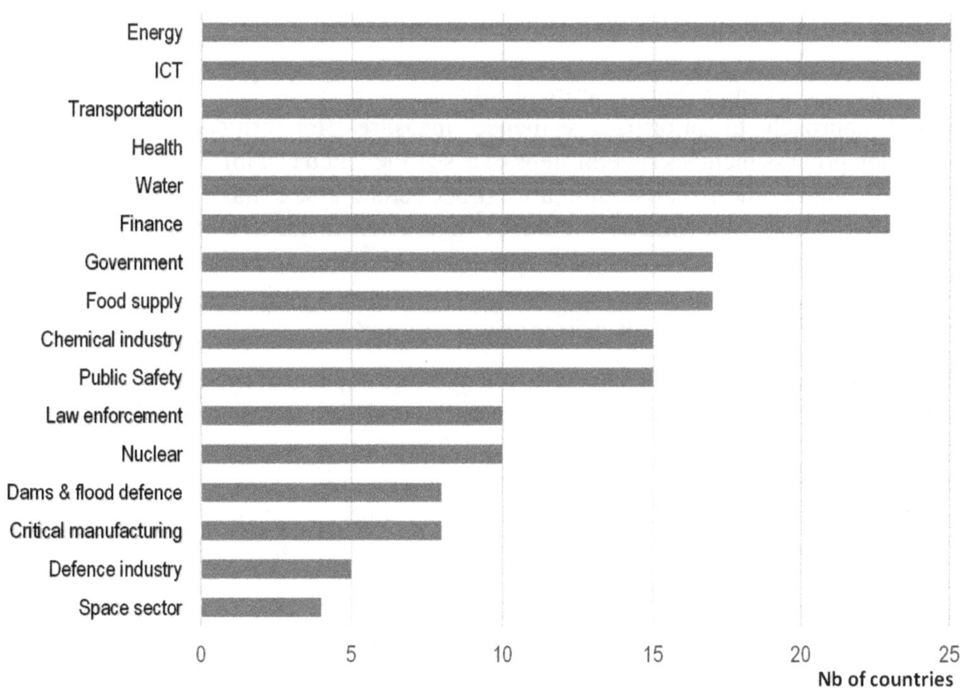

Note: Answers received from 25 OECD countries.
Source: OECD Survey on Critical Infrastructure Resilience and Security (2018)

Some countries have a large number of critical infrastructure sectors, like the United States with 16 different sectors (White House, 2013[43]). Other countries can limit their critical infrastructure policy to two sectors only, such as Portugal, with only electricity and transportation considered as critical infrastructure sectors as per the provisions of the 2008 Directive of the European Council on the identification and designation of European critical infrastructures and the assessment of the need to improve their protection (European Council, 2008[44]).

Overall, six sectors are widely classified as being critical across OECD countries: information and communication technologies, energy, finance, health, transport and water. A second group of sectors, including government, food supply, chemical industry, or public safety, is mentioned as critical in at least half of the responding countries. Other sectors appear to be more country-specific. This includes law enforcement, nuclear, dams and food defence, critical manufacturing, the defence industry of the space sector that are not considered as critical for the functioning of society for a vast majority of countries critical infrastructure policies.

Similar to the generic definition of critical infrastructure, the list of critical sectors can evolve over time to address emerging vulnerabilities and evolving risks. Some countries also have decided to define general sectors as well as sub-sectors of critical infrastructures, which leads to differences in categorisation across countries. For example, Switzerland does not provide a separate category for the nuclear sector as would be the case in the United States, instead it is a sub-category in the energy supply and distribution sector. While these differences reflect national preferences, it can be important to better harmonise approaches across countries especially to favour transboundary and international cooperation on this policy issue.

Identifying critical assets and assessing their vulnerabilities

The next step of a comprehensive critical infrastructure policy is to define a systematic analytical approach to prioritise resilience measures for critical infrastructure. A prioritisation process includes several steps of assessment and can inform targeted planning and investment decisions. First, not all infrastructure assets have the same level of criticality. Criticality assessments should be conducted to identify assets, systems, and networks that are truly critical (DHS, 2013[45]); (Theocharidou and Giannopoulos, 2015[46]).

Identifying critical assets with criticality assessment

Criticality analysis should include an assessment of the impacts of the critical infrastructure disruption on a range of pre-established criteria. Several approaches are used across OECD countries. For instance, in Switzerland a first differentiation is done between the different sectors and sub-sectors with three categories of criticality (very high criticality, high criticality, normal criticality). In the Netherlands, economic, physical and social criteria enable to define the different critical infrastructure processes, but then a distinction is made between category A where disruptions can have large impacts and cascading effects and category B where impacts can be lower, in order to reflect the diversity within critical infrastructure and to set priorities. In terms of criteria, the European Commission defines a minimum set for critical infrastructure assessment, including public impacts, economic impacts, environmental impacts, interdependence, political impacts and psychological impacts (European Council, 2008[44]).

The important point in criticality assessment is to include an interdependency assessment, in order to identify the critical points of a system, or between different sectors that are essential to keep running when a crisis occurs to avoid cascading failures. Critical infrastructure dependencies and interdependencies can be physical when the state of one infrastructure is dependent on the material output of the other, but there can also be digital, geographic or logical dependencies to be considered in such assessment (Rinaldi, Peerenboom and Kelly, 2001[47]); (Macaulay, 2009[48]). Against this backdrop, it is important to develop models to estimate service loss, which requires to map out the functional links between infrastructure systems.

While interdependency analysis is an area where research is making significant progress, methodologies are not yet widely utilised across OECD countries: only 36% of the respondents to the OECD Survey indicated that they had identified dependencies (Figure 3.2). Argonne National Laboratory in the United States provides a useful overview on the different methods that governments and operators can use for such interdependency assessment of critical infrastructure (Petit et al., 2015[49]).

Figure 3.2. Mapping of critical infrastructure interdependencies across OECD countries

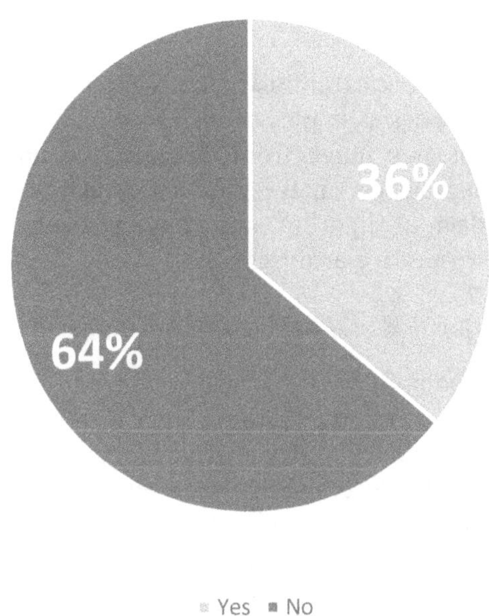

Note: Response to the question "Has your central government mapped interdependencies between different sectors of critical infrastructure?" across the 25 respondents to the OECD Survey
Source: OECD Survey on Critical Infrastructure Resilience and Security (2018)

Criticality assessment usually leads to the development of critical assets inventories, registers or maps, with different levels of classification according to their criticality. Most of the countries which have established critical infrastructure programmes and strategies, have set-up such inventories. For instance, in France, critical infrastructure are precisely referenced and located by the General Secretariat on Defence and national Security, and an effort to focus on the most critical ones led to reducing their number from more than 7000 to around 1500. There are also examples of transboundary mapping of critical infrastructure, such as at the European Union level, in the context of the EU Directive 2008/114/EC on identification and designation of European critical infrastructures and assessment of the need to improve their protection.

Conducting vulnerability analysis to identify weak points

Once critical assets are mapped out and hierarchically classified, vulnerability assessments enable identifying weak points where potential failures are likely to happen. A thorough vulnerability assessment of critical infrastructure provides insight into the most important risks, threats, vulnerabilities and degree of resilience of this infrastructure. To do so, it is fundamental to stress test critical infrastructure vulnerability to a series of risk scenarios of different likelihood, magnitude, or their combination, across a range of potential hazards and threats. These assessments consider the most likely scenarios, in addition to those that are less probable, but might nonetheless materialize.

A holistic, all-hazards approach can help uncover complex vulnerabilities. Canada's national strategy for critical infrastructure equally stresses the need for an all-hazards risk analysis that takes accidental, intentional and natural hazards into account ((Public Safety Canada, 2014[50])). It can be important also to integrate the vulnerabilities of governance systems of critical infrastructure in the analysis, as management failures during crises are all too common. The European Commission Joint Research Centre for instance has developed a stress-testing tool that focuses on these complex governance aspects with application in the nuclear and banking sectors. (Galbusera, Giannopoulos and Ward, 2014[51]).

Vulnerability assessments for critical infrastructures can be performed using a variety of methodologies. Box 3.1 provides examples of such methodologies from a series of OECD countries. These methodologies range from deterministic approaches to probabilistic methods. Deterministic approaches analyse and interpret historical disaster events and available retrospective data in light of new developments. Disaster scenarios and simulations expand on retrospective analyses.

Risk assessment as the basis for resilience investments

The identification of weak points allows prioritising where to concentrate resilience efforts in existing infrastructure systems: on failure points that would have the most severe consequences. Such prioritization can inform targeted planning and investment decisions, such as what infrastructure should be hardened or relocated first, or what infrastructure should receive priority restoration in the aftermath of a disaster to ensure rapid recovery (Verner, Petit and Kihaek, 2017[52]).

Risk assessment can be complemented to evaluate the benefits of investments in resilience or security to reduce risks, for both existing infrastructure as well as for new projects. By comparing the benefits of different resilience measures in reducing risk of failures, risk-informed cost-benefit analysis can support decision-making and resilience investment decisions.

Box 3.1. Critical Infrastructure Risk Assessment Methodologies in OECD countries

Critical Infrastructures and Systems Risk and Resilience Assessment Methodology (CRISRRAM).

CRISRRAM is a methodology developed by the European Commission. It takes an all-hazards and systems of systems approach, addressing risks and vulnerabilities of critical infrastructure at asset level, system level and society level. To tackle the complexity of risk assessments, CRISRRAM takes a scenario-based approach and recommends the assessment of all relevant single- and multi-hazard scenarios. To select the appropriate scenarios, Threat Likelihood Assessments should be done.

RAMCAP-Plus

The RAMCAP-Plus methodology was developed by the American Society of Civil Engineers as an all-hazards risk and resilience assessment approach. It encompasses all infrastructures factoring in the dual objectives of protection and resilience. The seven steps in the methodology are: asset characterization; threat characterization; consequence analysis; vulnerability analysis; threat assessment; risk and resilience assessment; and risks and resilience management. The tool has been designed for use by critical infrastructure operators and decision-makers alike.

DHS Regional Resiliency Assessment Program (RRAP)

The Regional Resiliency Assessment Program (RRAP) is a cooperative assessment of specific critical infrastructure within a designated geographic area and a regional analysis of the surrounding infrastructure to address a range of infrastructure resilience issues that could have regionally and nationally significant consequences. These voluntary, non-regulatory RRAP projects are led by the US Department of Homeland Security and are selected each year by the Department with input and guidance from federal, state, and local partners. This approach is being replicated in Canada.

Source: (Giannopoulos, Filippini and Schimmer, 2012[53]); (Theocharidou and Giannopoulos, 2015[46])

Sharing information on risks and vulnerabilities

Most OECD countries have established information-sharing platforms

Governance arrangements for strengthening critical resilience highlight the need for partnerships and platforms for facilitating information sharing and exchange of knowledge. The commitment of governments and operators to engage in dialogue about these issues through institutionalized, regular meetings has proven useful to build mutual trust based on shared interest, as well as to foster regular information sharing, joint exercises, situation awareness, coordination of actions, mutual assistance, sharing of equipment and emergency stocks.

Several countries have developed programs and approaches to foster trust-based connections between government and private owners and operators. Technical solutions, such as information sharing and collaboration web-portals can serve as a secure environment where private- and public-sector stakeholders can easily and regularly exchange data, information, and good practices relevant to critical infrastructure resilience (Bach et al., 2013[25]); (Lewis, 2006[54])).

The OECD Survey shows that 80% of the respondents have established such information-sharing mechanisms or platforms, most often on a voluntary basis. Box 3.2 provides examples of successful critical infrastructure stakeholder engagement and secure information-sharing approaches.

Challenges for effective information-sharing

Although information-sharing presents many benefits for better understanding and exchange of expertise to increase resilience of critical infrastructure, there remain several prevalent challenges.

Ensuring the security of the information shared from owners and operators of critical infrastructure is an essential component for building mutual trust, as some of this information may be important for competitiveness in the market or their image. As operators might not always be inclined to share sensitive information about their vulnerabilities and/ or their critical dependencies outside of safe circles, ensuring mutual trust and security of information shared is an important aspect to foster dialogue and exchange.

Equally important is to focus on the quality and not quantity of information that is shared through these mechanisms. The more clear and precise the information shared is, the more added-value it can offer to building resilience of critical infrastructure. All parties across government and private sector should see the benefits of this information sharing practice from their respective sides. Filtering through massive amount of information is less effective than sharing the most important elements about the security of critical infrastructure. Good quality information can create incentives to boost resilience.

Operators might be reluctant to engage in such partnership if they fear it will lead to extra costs that they will have to finance, once their vulnerabilities are known. Similarly, the risk that competitors do not engage in the process and free-ride on the increased level of resilience that it would lead can cause difficulties for operators to engage. Minimum security standards can help ensure that there are no 'weakest links' that could jeopardise the overall security of the system while also overcoming underinvestment in resilience and the lack of willingness to engage.

Box 3.2. Critical Infrastructure Stakeholder Engagement and Information Sharing

Seeking to facilitate efficient and effective relationships across stakeholder groups with shared responsibility for critical infrastructure resilience, several countries have developed programs and approaches to foster trust-based connections between government and private owners and operators.

• *Australia's Trusted Information Sharing Network (TISN) for Critical Infrastructure Resilience*

The TISN provides a secure, non-competitive environment in which all critical infrastructure stakeholders can collaborate and engage in resilience building initiatives. The Network allows owners and operators across sector groups to regularly share information and cooperate within and across sectors to address security and business continuity challenges.

• *Canada Critical Infrastructure Gateway*

The Gateway meets one of the objectives under the Canadian National Strategy and Action Plan for Critical Infrastructure is the timely advancement of information sharing and protection among critical infrastructure partners. It is a collaborative, unclassified web-based workspace that includes members of the critical infrastructure community.

• *The European Union's Critical Infrastructure Warning Information Network (CIWIN)*

CIWIN is an information sharing system developed as a supporting component of the European Programme for critical Infrastructure Protection. The CIWIN facilitates the exchange of information on shared threats, vulnerabilities and appropriate measures and strategies to mitigate risk to critical infrastructure among European Union members and the European Commission. In addition to its information-sharing function, the CIWIN serves as a rapid alert system for early warnings regarding acute risks and threats.

• *United States Information Sharing and Analysis Centers (ISACs)*

Sector-specific ISACs may be extensions of the national-level government, as in the case of the U.S. Telecommunications ISAC, which is managed by the National Communications System within the U.S. Department of Homeland Security, or entirely run by industry as the is the U.S. Water ISAC, a non-profit extension of the water sector's professional society. ISACs are viewed as a source for security-related best practices and for hazard and threat indications, warnings, and assessments.

• *United States Department of Homeland Security Protective Security Advisor (PSA) Program*

The program provides for proactive engagement among government partners and private sector owners and operators with responsibility for critical infrastructure. PSAs plan, coordinate, and conduct security and resilience surveys and assessments of nationally significant critical infrastructure. The program also delivers outreach activities and provides owners, operators, and other stakeholders with access to critical infrastructure security and resilience resources, training, and information. During and after an incident, Advisors serve as liaisons between government officials and private sector critical infrastructure owners and operators.

Sources: Australian Government, Trusted Information Sharing Network, http://www.tisn.gov.au ; Canadian Critical Infrastructure Information Gateway, https://cigateways.ps.gc.ca ; EU Critical Infrastructure Warning Information Network, http://ec.europa.eu/dgs/home-affairs/what-we-do/networks/critical_infrastructure_warning_information_network/index_en.htm ; U.S. Department of Homeland Security, Partnering for Critical Infrastructure Security and Resilience, https://www.dhs.gov/publication/nipp-2013-partnering-critical-infrastructure-security-and-resilience; US DHS, Protective Security Advisors, https://www.dhs.gov/protective-security-advisors

Prioritising resilience measures and policy instruments

A large variety of policy tool to foster operators' resilience investments exists

Strengthening resilience to critical infrastructure is a collaborative effort amongst several stakeholders requiring a mix of tools to gather information, prioritise resilience investments, and increase overall incentives.

Governments can choose from a variety of policy tools and mechanisms to strengthen critical infrastructure resilience. Instruments range from prescriptive regulatory tools, compensation mechanisms, to voluntary frameworks based on partnerships between government and operators. Twenty-two policy tools have been identified in the OECD Survey on critical infrastructure resilience (Table 3.1). These policy tools are further described in Annex 3.D. This comprehensive list aims to present the different policy options that government can use, once they have set up a critical infrastructure resilience programme, identified its most critical infrastructure and their vulnerability, and established an information sharing mechanism with critical infrastructure operators.

Table 3.1. Policy tools to foster critical infrastructure resilience

1. Provision of hazards and threats information	12. Inspections and performance assessments
2. Voluntary information-sharing mechanisms or platforms	13. Fines for non-compliance with resilience requirements
3. Mandatory information-sharing mechanisms or platforms	14. Other types of penalties for non-compliance
4. Awareness raising activities and trainings	15. Ranking based on inspection / performance results
5. Resilience guidelines for critical infrastructure operators	16. Reporting on operators resilience
6. Fostering the development/use of professional standards	17. Sharing best practices
7. Incentive mechanism to assess risks and vulnerabilities	18. Public investments in infrastructure resilience
8. Incentive mechanisms for investing in resilience	19. Guidance for sub-national levels of government
9. Sectoral prescriptive regulations dedicated to CIP	20. Mandatory insurance for critical infrastructure
10. Performance-based regulations on business continuity	21. Peer-reviews, monitoring and evaluation
11. Mandatory business continuity plans	22. Sectoral mutual aid agreements

Note: This listing of policy tools was prepared by the OECD Secretariat, based on approaches presented at the OECD High Level Risk Forum and desk research
Source: OECD Secretariat

Identifying the pros and cons of these different tools in different policy contexts can be of great support for designing critical infrastructure protection and resilience policies. The OECD High Level Risk Forum, through its survey and case studies has initiated taking stocks of these policy tools. The following considerations can contribute to facilitating the choices that governments can make amongst these different options.

Regulation is an important method that provides mandatory requirements and enforcement mechanisms for critical infrastructure resilience. The regulatory approach has strengths in that it provides mandatory requirements, but it can also prove costly and create lags of time between technological developments in many sectors that require regular updates. Different regulatory approaches can be applied from prescriptive sectoral regulations to performance-based ones, which let operators define by themselves the way to achieve resilience targets.

Financial incentives provide another method to increase investments and continuity plans for critical infrastructure protection and resilience. The design of compensation mechanisms for customers in case of service disruption or other types of penalties can be used to internalise the benefits of resilience. This provides operators with the choice of the ways to increase their resilience. In Finland, the 2013 Energy Market Act provides such an incentive structure for electricity distribution operators to invest in the resilience of their network, with the combination of price incentives for improved resilience with important fees in case resilience targets are not attained (Chapter 4).

Public finance used for critical infrastructure resilience can set standards and demonstrate the value of up-front investments in resilience. Integrating resilience in major public investment projects sets an example for value and benefits of these investments, and can create incentives for other critical infrastructure owners and operators to follow suit (OECD, 2018[12]). Public procurement is increasingly factoring in climate resilience, which can serve as an approach to expand to other risks as well. For example, the Greater Paris 30 billion euro investment in public transportation was designed with specific flood resilience requirements beyond the existing regulation (OECD, 2014[7]).

Peer-pressure is another policy option that works amongst owners and operators of critical infrastructure based on holding up their image and rankings to the public. Creating public access to evaluations of critical infrastructure creates concerns for companies and their image. Rankings are important indicators of resiliency and an incentive-creating mechanism. Korea has included a mechanism of peer-pressure within its system for managing the failure of infrastructure. Every year, the Periodic Nationwide Safety Diagnosis makes a sampling diagnosis for 21 types of infrastructures. These evaluations are made public and provide rankings of the infrastructure, creating important incentives for companies to keep up their public image. Another example is found with the National Emergency Supply Agency (NESA) in Finland. The annual assessments of the business continuity plans of operators in the energy sector is presented to the pool of operators so that they can compare their performance and learn from each other (See chapter 4). While in this case, the results are not publicly disclosed, peer-pressure within the sector provides incentives for improving performance. The increasing public disclosure of climate risks can here also provide elements of reflection for critical infrastructure resilience to multiple hazards (OECD, 2018[12])

Finding the right combination between mandatory and voluntary frameworks

It is important for governments to find the right combination between mandatory and voluntary frameworks to enhance stakeholder engagement in resilience. As shown in Figure 3.3, the results of the OECD survey indicate a preference towards voluntary frameworks to strengthen critical infrastructure resilience.

Instruments such as guidance for sub-national levels of governments, awareness raiding activities and trainings, provision of hazards and threats information, resilience guidelines for critical infrastructure operators and voluntary information sharing mechanism are the policy tools that are the most commonly used by OECD governments. On the contrary, more stringent tools, such as inspections and performance assessments, sectoral prescriptive regulations, or mandatory business continuity plans, are less utilised by OECD countries to foster critical infrastructure resilience.

This preference for voluntary frameworks demonstrates that overall, critical infrastructure resilience policies are still at an early age in many OECD countries. In that context, operators' engagement in broad multi-stakeholders partnerships with governments remains a key priority, which enables building trust between the public and the private sector. Adopting voluntary frameworks appears to be more effective to achieve this objective.

Nevertheless, this approach does not necessarily guarantee a strong enough incentive structure to ensure that sufficient investments are effectively made to attain expected resilience targets. Over the years, once the value of these partnerships will be widely acknowledged, one can expect that mandatory approaches will be more easily accepted and more largely developed, in order to guarantee that operators ensure some forms of minimum common standards of resilience. The OECD Policy Toolkit on the Governance of Critical Infrastructure Resilience proposed in Chapter 5 provides a way forward for governments aiming to strengthen progressively the resilience of critical infrastructure in their country with a staged approach based on partnerships.

Figure 3.3. Policy tools for critical infrastructure resilience across OECD countries

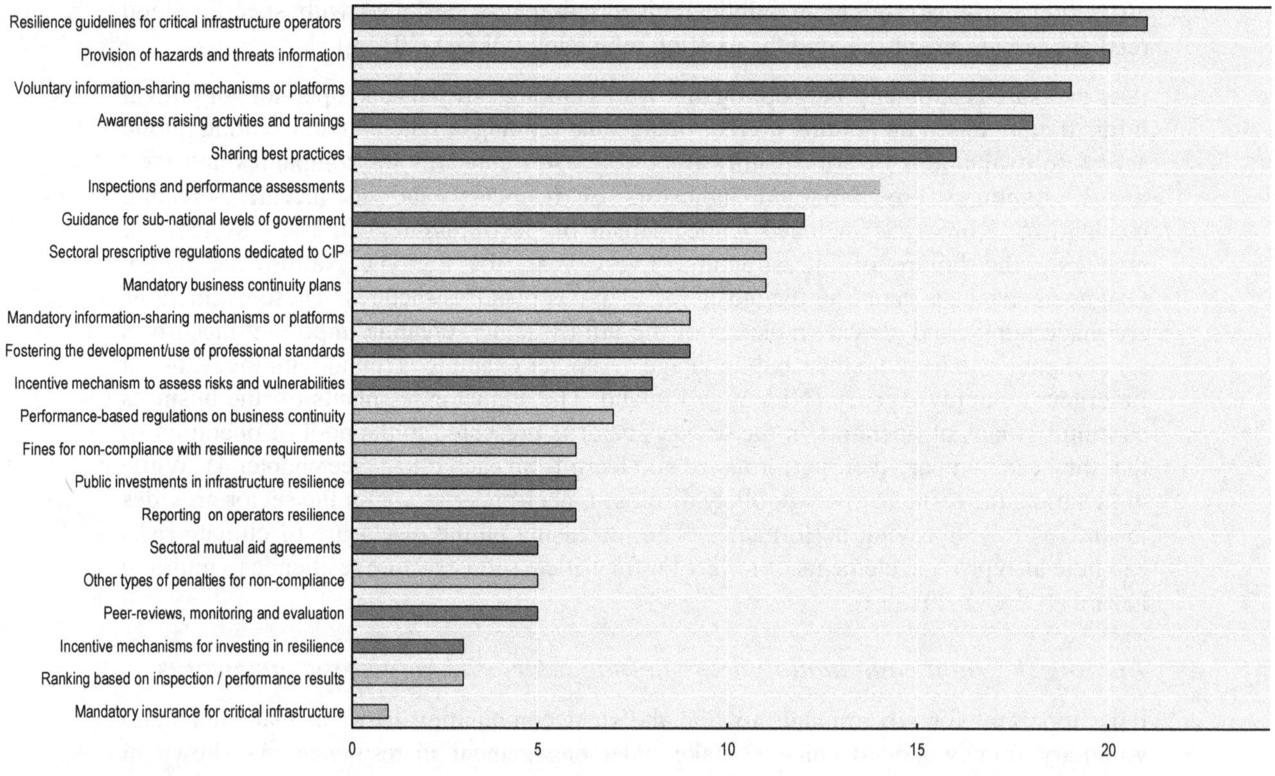

Resilience guidelines for critical infrastructure operators
Provision of hazards and threats information
Voluntary information-sharing mechanisms or platforms
Awareness raising activities and trainings
Sharing best practices
Inspections and performance assessments
Guidance for sub-national levels of government
Sectoral prescriptive regulations dedicated to CIP
Mandatory business continuity plans
Mandatory information-sharing mechanisms or platforms
Fostering the development/use of professional standards
Incentive mechanism to assess risks and vulnerabilities
Performance-based regulations on business continuity
Fines for non-compliance with resilience requirements
Public investments in infrastructure resilience
Reporting on operators resilience
Sectoral mutual aid agreements
Other types of penalties for non-compliance
Peer-reviews, monitoring and evaluation
Incentive mechanisms for investing in resilience
Ranking based on inspection / performance results
Mandatory insurance for critical infrastructure
0 5 10 15 20

Note: 22 OECD countries responded to the survey as of 10 September 2018 – mandatory tools are in grey, voluntary tools are in blue.
Source: OECD Survey on Critical Infrastructure Resilience (2018)

Cost-sharing arrangements for resilient investments

Operators have a keen interest in maintaining the continuity of their services and their reputation by investing in resilience. However, investments in resilience often imply costs up front, even if these should be compensated in terms of greater reliability of service and resilience to shocks.

The question is how to find the right balance. Excessive requirements imposed by governments to strengthen resilience can result in additional costs of service borne by customers, citizens and businesses. When deciding on the policy tools best fitted to improve critical infrastructure resilience in their national contexts, governments should assess how these different options can provide effective incentives for operators to invest in resilience, while managing the repercussions on the cost of service. Solving this economic equation is the cornerstone for an efficient policy, but there is no simple solution. As shown in the Finland case-study in Chapter 4, engaging in trusted partnerships and regular dialogue between governments, regulators and operators should enable discussing cost-sharing arrangements to attain resilience objectives.

References

Bach, C. et al. (2013), "Adding value to critical infrastructure research and disaster risk management: the resilience concept", *http://journals.openedition.org/sapiens* 6.1, https://journals.openedition.org/sapiens/1626 (accessed on 25 February 2019). [25]

Barami, B. (2013), *Infrastructure Resiliency: A Risk-Based Framework*, US Department of Transportation, https://www.volpe.dot.gov/sites/volpe.dot.gov/files/docs/Infrastructure%20Resiliency_A%20Risk-Based%20Framework.pdf (accessed on 25 February 2019). [36]

Chang, S. et al. (2014), "Toward Disaster-Resilient Cities: Characterizing Resilience of Infrastructure Systems with Expert Judgments", *Risk Analysis*, Vol. 34/3, pp. 416-434, http://dx.doi.org/10.1111/risa.12133. [37]

Critical Five (2014), *Forging a Common Understanding for Critical Infrastructure Shared Narrative*, https://www.dhs.gov/sites/default/files/publications/critical-five-shared-narrative-critical-infrastructure-2014-508.pdf (accessed on 25 February 2019). [34]

DHS (2013), *NIPP 2013: Partnering for Critical Infrastructure Security and Resilience | Homeland Security*, https://www.dhs.gov/publication/nipp-2013-partnering-critical-infrastructure-security-and-resilience (accessed on 25 February 2019). [45]

European Council (2008), *COUNCIL DIRECTIVE 2008/114/EC of 8 December 2008 on the identification and designation of European critical infrastructures and the assessment of the need to improve their protection*, https://eur-lex.europa.eu/LexUriServ/LexUriServ.do?uri=OJ:L:2008:345:0075:0082:EN:PDF (accessed on 26 February 2019). [44]

Flynn, S. (2015), *Bolstering Critical Infrastructure Resilience After Superstorm Sandy: Lessons for New York and the Nation*, Northeastern University, Boston, Massachusetts, http://dx.doi.org/10.17760/D20241717. [19]

Flynn, S. (2008), "America the Resilient, Defying Terrorism and Mitigating Natural Disasters", *Foreign Affairs*, https://www.foreignaffairs.com/articles/2008-03-02/america-resilient (accessed on 25 February 2019). [35]

Galbusera, L., G. Giannopoulos and D. Ward (2014), *Developing stress tests to improve the resilience of critical infrastructures: a feasibility analysis*, European Commission Joint Research Centre, http://dx.doi.org/10.2788/954065. [51]

Giannopoulos, G., R. Filippini and M. Schimmer (2012), *Risk assessment methodologies for Critical Infrastructure Protection. Part I: A state of the art*, European Commission Joint Research Centre, http://dx.doi.org/10.2788/22260. [53]

Lewis, T. (2006), *Critical infrastructure protection in homeland security : defending a networked nation*, Wiley-Interscience. [54]

Macaulay, T. (2009), *Critical infrastructure : understanding its component parts, vulnerabilities, operating risks, and interdependencies*, CRC Press, https://www.crcpress.com/Critical-Infrastructure-Understanding-Its-Component-Parts-Vulnerabilities/Macaulay/p/book/9781420068351 (accessed on 26 February 2019). [48]

Moteff, J. (2012), *CRS Report for Congress Critical Infrastructure Resilience: The Evolution of Policy and Programs and Issues for Congress*, Congressional Research Service, https://fas.org/sgp/crs/homesec/R42683.pdf (accessed on 25 February 2019). [42]

OECD (2018), *Assessing Global Progress in the Governance of Critical Risks*, OECD Reviews of Risk Management Policies, OECD Publishing, Paris, https://dx.doi.org/10.1787/9789264309272-en. [2]

OECD (2018), "Climate-resilient Infrastructure", *OECD Environment Policy Paper*, No. 14, OECD, Paris, http://www.oecd.org/environment/cc/policy-perspectives-climate-resilient-infrastructure.pdf (accessed on 25 February 2019). [12]

OECD (2014), *Seine Basin, Île-de-France, 2014: Resilience to Major Floods*, OECD Reviews of Risk Management Policies, OECD Publishing, Paris, https://dx.doi.org/10.1787/9789264208728-en. [7]

OECD (2011), *Future Global Shocks: Improving Risk Governance*, OECD Reviews of Risk Management Policies, OECD Publishing, Paris, https://dx.doi.org/10.1787/9789264114586-en. [9]

OECD and EU JRC (2018), *System thinking for critical infrastructure resilience and security - OECD/ JRC Workshop - OECD*, http://www.oecd.org/gov/risk/workshop-oecd-jrc-system-thinking-for-critical-infrastructure-resilience-and-security.htm (accessed on 25 February 2019). [41]

Petit, F. et al. (2015), *Analysis of Critical Infrastructure Dependencies and Interdependencies*, Argonne National Laboratory, https://publications.anl.gov/anlpubs/2015/06/111906.pdf (accessed on 26 February 2019). [49]

Public Safety Canada (2014), *Action Plan for Critical Infrastructure 2014-2017*, https://www.publicsafety.gc.ca/cnt/rsrcs/pblctns/pln-crtcl-nfrstrctr-2014-17/pln-crtcl-nfrstrctr-2014-17-eng.pdf (accessed on 26 February 2019). [50]

Rinaldi, S., J. Peerenboom and T. Kelly (2001), *Identifying, Understanding, and Analyzing Critical Infrastructure Interdependencies*, https://pdfs.semanticscholar.org/b1b7/d1e0bb39badc3592373427840a4039d9717d.pdf (accessed on 26 February 2019). [47]

Theocharidou, M. and G. Giannopoulos (2015), "Risk assessment methodologies for critical infrastructure protection. Part II: A new approach", http://dx.doi.org/10.2788/621843. [46]

Verner, D., F. Petit and K. Kihaek (2017), "Incorporating Prioritization in Critical Infrastructure Security and Resilience Programs - HOMELAND SECURITY AFFAIRS", *Homeland Security Affaits*, Vol. 13, https://www.hsaj.org/articles/14091 (accessed on 26 February 2019). [52]

White House (2013), *Presidential Policy Directive -- Critical Infrastructure Security and Resilience | whitehouse.gov*, https://obamawhitehouse.archives.gov/the-press-office/2013/02/12/presidential-policy-directive-critical-infrastructure-security-and-resil (accessed on 25 February 2019). [43]

Annex 3.A. Critical infrastructure strategy or programme and lead institution in charge

Country	Y/N*	Critical infrastructure strategy or programme	Lead institution in charge
Australia	Yes	Critical Infrastructure Resilience Strategy (2015) https://www.tisn.gov.au/Documents/CriticalInfrastructureResilienceStrategyPlan.PDF	Attorney-General's Department / Critical Infrastructure Centre
Austria	Yes	Austrian Program for Critical Infrastructure Protection –Masterplan 2014 http://archiv.bundeskanzleramt.at/DocView.axd?CobId=58907	Federal Chancellery Federal Ministry of the Interior
Belgium	Yes	Belgium Critical Infrastructure Protection Strategy https://crisiscentrum.be/nl/inhoud/kritieke-infrastructuur-0	Federal Public Service Home Affairs, National Crisis Centre (directorate CIPRA)
Canada	Yes	National Strategy for Critical Infrastructure www.publicsafety.gc.ca/cnt/ntnl-scrt/crtcl-nfrstrctr/index-en.aspx	Public Safety Canada
Chile	No		
Czech Republic	Yes	National Programme for Critical Infrastructure Protection (2010), Comprehensive strategy of the Czech Republic for Critical Infrastructure (2010) -	Ministry of the Interior of the Czech Republic
Denmark	No		
Estonia	Yes	Internal Security Development Plan 2015 – 2020 https://valitsus.ee/sites/default/files/content-editors/arengukavad/taiendatud_siseturvalisuse_arengukava_2015-2020.pdf	Ministry of the Interior
Finland	Yes	Government decision on the security of supply (2013) https://www.nesa.fi/security-of-supply/objectives/	National Emergency Supply Agency http://www.nesa.fi/
France	Yes	Instruction générale interministérielle relative à la sécurité des activités d'importance vitale http://circulaire.legifrance.gouv.fr/pdf/2014/01/cir_37828.pdf Critical infrastructure protection strategy defined in the law (defence code – articles L. 1332-1 to L. 1332-7, R. 1332-1 to R. 1332-42	Secrétariat Général de la Défense et de la Sécurité Nationale (SGDSN) www.sgdsn.fr
Germany	Yes	National Strategy for Critical Infrastructure Protection (2009) https://www.bmi.bund.de/SharedDocs/downloads/EN/publikationen/2009/kritis_englisch.pdf?__blob=publicationFile&v=1	Federal Ministry of Interior
Greece	Yes		
Hungary	N/A		
Iceland	Yes		
Ireland	Yes		
Israel	Yes		National Emergency Management Authority in the Ministry of Defense
Italy	N/A		
Japan	No		
Korea	Yes	National Infrastructure Protection Plan https://opengov.seoul.go.kr/sanction/10812531	Ministry of the Interior and Safety (MOIS)
Latvia	Yes	Procedures for the identification of critical infrastructures Cabinet of Ministers Regulation No. 496, adopted on 1 June 2010 http://likumi.lv/doc.php?id=212031 ; Procedures for planning and implementation of security measures for the critical infrastructure Regulation No. 100 (2017) http://likumi.lv/doc.php?id=225776 Regulation on Civil Protection plans structure Cabinet of Ministers Regulation No. 658, adopted on 7 November 2017 https://likumi.lv/ta/id/294938-noteikumi-par-civilas-aizsardzibas-planu-strukturu-un-tajos-ieklaujamo-informaciju	National Security Interinstitutional Commission Secretariat: Ministry of Interior

Luxembourg	Yes	Grand-ducal regulation of 21 February 2018 laying down the identification and designation of critical infrastructure http://data.legilux.public.lu/eli/etat/leg/rgd/2018/02/21/a152/jo Grand-ducal regulation of 21 February 2018 specifying the structure for security and business continuity plans of critical infrastructure http://data.legilux.public.lu/eli/etat/leg/rgd/2018/02/21/a151/jo	High Commission for National Protection https://hcpn.gouvernement.lu/en/service/attributions.html
Mexico	Yes		
Netherlands	Yes	Critical Infrastructure Protection, January 2018 https://english.nctv.nl/binaries/Factsheet%20Vitaal%20ENG%202016%20(web)_tcm32-240750.pdf	National Coordinator for Security and Counterterrorism (NCTV)https://english.nctv.nl/
New Zealand	Yes	Obligations on infrastructure providers are required by the Civil Defence Emergency Management Act 2002 and secondary legislation including the National Civil Defence Emergency Management Plan Order 2015 and Guidance, specifically "Lifeline Utilities and CDEM – Director's Guideline for Lifeline Utilities and Civil Defence Emergency Management Groups" [DGL 16/14]. The Thirty Year New Zealand Infrastructure Plan 2015 sets out central Government's long-term vision for infrastructure to be resilient, coordinated and contributing to a strong economy and high living standards.	The Ministry of Civil Defence and Emergency Management (MCDEM)
Norway	Yes	Vital functions in society https://www.dsb.no/globalassets/dokumenter/rapporter/kiks-ii_english_version.pdf	Directorate for Civil Protection (DSB) https://www.dsb.no/menyartikler/english/
Poland	Yes	The National Critical Infrastructure Protection Programme http://rcb.gov.pl/wp-content/uploads/NPOIK-2015_eng-1.pdf	Government Security Center (RCB)
Portugal	No	There is no specific national programme or strategy, but there is the national regulation on CIP (Law-Decree 62/2011, of 9th May) http://www.prociv.pt/bk/RISCOSPREV/INFRAESTRUTURASCRITICAS/Documents/DL_62_2011_identificacao_e_protecao_de_infraestruturas_essenciais.pdf	National Authority for Civil Protection (ANPC) the Internal Security System (SSI)
Slovak Republic	No	Act on Critical Infrastructure No 45/2011	Ministry of Interior
Slovenia	Yes		
Spain	Yes	Law 8/2011 of 28 April, "Establishing measures for the protection of critical infrastructures" and Royal Decree 704/2011 of 20 May http://www.cnpic.es/ National Plan for Critical Infrastructure Protection (updated in February 2016 – Classified information) Spanish Critical Infrastructure Protection Planning System (classified) http://www.cnpic.es/en/Preguntas_Frecuentes/que_es_el_sistema_de_planificacion_PIC/index.html	National Center for Infrastructure Protection & Cybersecurity (CNPIC)
Sweden	Yes	Action Plan for the Protection of Vital Societal Functions & Critical Infrastructure https://www.msb.se/RibData/Filer/pdf/27412.pdf	Swedish Civil Contingencies Agency (MSB)
Switzerland	Yes	New CIP strategy to be adopted by Federal Council on December 8, 2017 www.infraprotection.ch	Federal Office for Civil Protection (FOCP)
Turkey	Yes	2014-2023 Technological Disasters Roadmap Document 2018-2022 AFAD Strategic Plan	Disaster and Emergency Management Presidency
United Kingdom	Yes	2015 National Security Strategy and Strategic Defence and Security Review http://www.cpni.gov.uk/about/cni/	Centre for the Protection of National Infrastructure (CPNI) National Cyber Security Centre (NCSC)
United States	Yes	NIPP 2013: Partnering for Critical Infrastructure Security and Resilience and 2015 Sector-Specific Plans https://www.dhs.gov/2015-sector-specific-plans	Department of Homeland Security (DHS)

*: Yes or No response to the question "Has your national government adopted a critical infrastructure strategy or programme?"

Annex 3.B. Definition of Critical Infrastructure in OECD countries

Country	Official definition of critical infrastructure
Australia	Those physical facilities, supply chains, information technologies and communication networks which, if destroyed, degraded or rendered unavailable for an extended period, would significantly impact the social or economic wellbeing of the nation or affect Australia's ability to conduct national defence and ensure national security Source: Critical Infrastructure Resilience Strategy (2010) and Critical Infrastructure Resilience Strategy: Plan (2015)
Austria	Critical infrastructures are those infrastructures (systems, facilities, processes, networks or parts thereof) that are essential for the maintenance of important social functions and whose disruption or destruction seriously affects the health, safety or economic and social well-being of large parts of the population or the effective functioning of state institutions Source: http://archiv.bundeskanzleramt.at/DocView.axd?CobId=58907
Belgium	A critical infrastructure is being defined in Belgian law as "an asset, system or part thereof, of federal importance, which is essential for the maintenance of vital societal functions, health, safety, security, economic or social well-being of people, and the disruption or destruction of which would have a significant impact as a result of the failure to maintain those functions" Source: https://crisiscentrum.be/sites/default/files/loi_du_1er_juillet_2011_sur_les_ic.pdf
Canada	Critical infrastructure refers to processes, systems, facilities, technologies, networks, assets and services essential to the health, safety, security or economic well-being of Canadians and the effective functioning of government. Source: National Strategy for Critical Infrastructure (2009) and Action Plan for Critical Infrastructure 2014-2017
Czech Republic	Critical infrastructure shall denote the element of critical infrastructure or the system of elements of critical infrastructure, disruption of which would have a significant impact on the State security, on ensuring the basic living needs of the population, on health of people and State economy - (CRISIS MANAGEMENT ACT N. 240/2000 Coll).
Estonia	Adopt same definition as the European Council Directive 2008. In addition, Estonia has introduced the term "vital service" into domestic legislation. A vital service is a service that has an overwhelming impact on the functioning of society and the interruption of which is an immediate threat to the life or health of people or to the operation of another vital service or service of general interest. A vital service is regarded in its entirety together with a building, piece of equipment, staff, reserves and other similar facilities indispensable to the operation of the vital service. Source: Republic of Estonia Information System Authority https://www.ria.ee/en/ciip.html
European Union	Critical infrastructure 'means an asset, system or part thereof located in Member States which is essential for the maintenance of vital societal functions, health, safety, security, economic or social well-being of people, and the disruption or destruction of which would have a significant impact in a Member State as a result of the failure to maintain those functions. European critical infrastructure' or 'ECI' means critical infrastructure located in Member States the disruption or destruction of which would have a significant impact on at least two Member States. Source: Council Directive 2008/114/EC
France	The institutions, structures or facilities that provide the essential goods and services forming the backbone of French society and its way of life Source: General Secretariat for Defence and National Security (SGDSN), January 2017 http://cache.media.education.gouv.fr/file/2017/54/5/SGDSN-PLAQUETTE_SAIV_ANG_12012017_763545.pdf
Finland	Infrastructures that are most crucial to the functioning of society are called critical infrastructures. In the Security Strategy for Society, critical infrastructures are defined as the structures and functions that are vital for the continuous functioning of society. Critical infrastructure includes physical facilities and structures as well as online functions and services Source: The Security Committee, 2015; https://www.turvallisuuskomitea.fi/index.php/fi/files/26/.../Secure%20Finland.pdf

Germany	Critical infrastructures (CI) are organizational and physical structures and facilities of such vital importance to a nation's society and economy that their failure or degradation would result in sustained supply shortages, significant disruption of public safety and security, or other dramatic consequences. Source: National Strategy for Critical Infrastructure Protection (2009)
Israel	A complex of buildings and infrastructure, technological systems, logistical equipment, computing and communications systems, that are institutionally activated and controlled, that provides a vital service to the population and economy. Source: 2017 OECD High Level Risk Forum Critical Infrastructure Questionnaire
Korea	National infrastructure implies that the facilities are deemed necessary to be continuously managed to protect the national infrastructure, according to the following standards, 1. Ripple effects on other infrastructure, systems, etc.; 2. Necessity for at least two central administrative agencies to jointly respond to disasters; 3. The scale and scope of damage that is caused by any disaster to the national security, the economy, and the society; 4. The possibility that a disaster can occur and the easiness of recovering from such disaster. Source: Framework Act on the Management of Disasters and Safety
Latvia	Objects, systems or parts of systems located on the territory of Republic of Latvia, which are important for implementation of functions vital to society and for provision of health protection, security, economic and social welfare, and destruction or malfunction of which would significantly affect the functions of the State. Source: National Security Law, 2010
Luxembourg	Critical infrastructure means any point, system or part of it which is indispensable for the safeguarding of vital interests or essential needs of all or part of the country or population or which is likely to be subject to a particular threat Source: Loi 23 juillet, 2016 http://legilux.public.lu/eli/etat/leg/memorial/2016/137
Mexico	Strategic infrastructure is defined as infrastructure that is indispensable for the provision of public goods and services and whose destruction or disruption is a threat to national security.
Netherlands	Certain processes are very critical for the Dutch society. The failure or disruption of such processes would result in severe social disruption and poses a threat to national security. These processes together form the critical infrastructure of The Netherlands. Source: National Coordinator for Security and Counterterrorism, January 2018, https://english.nctv.nl/binaries/Factsheet%20Critical%20Infrastructure%20ENG%202018_tcm32-240750.pdf
New Zealand	Critical infrastructure, also referred to as nationally significant infrastructure, can be broadly defined as the systems, assets, facilities and networks that provide essential services and are necessary for the national security, economic security, prosperity, and health and safety of their respective nations. Source: Critical 5 – Forging a Common Understanding for Critical Infrastructure, shared narrative, March 2014, New Zealand treasury.
Norway	Critical infrastructure is the facilities and systems that are absolutely necessary to maintain the community's critical functions which again covers society's basic needs and the population sense of security Source: OECD Survey on critical infrastructure (2017)
Poland	The Act of 26 April 2007 on Crisis Management (Dz. U. [Journal of Laws] of 2013, item 1166 and of 2015, item 1485 – hereinafter referred to as: "the Act on Crisis Management") defines the critical infrastructure as the systems and functional sites forming their part which are mutually related, such as building sites, facilities, installations, key services for the safety of the state and its citizens and serving to ensure efficient functioning of the public administration authorities, as well as institutions and entrepreneurs Source: National Critical Infrastructure Protection Programme Poland, 2015
Portugal	Critical Infrastructure is the component, system or part thereof, which is essential for the maintenance of vital functions to society, health, safety and economic or social well-being and whose disruption or destruction would have a significant impact, given the circumstance that the infrastructure will be unable to continue performing those functions. Source: OECD Survey on critical infrastructure (2017)

Slovak Republic	a) Critical infrastructure element (hereinafter referred to as the "element") means mainly an engineering building, public service and information system in the critical infrastructure sector whose disruption or destruction should, according to the sectoral criteria and cross-cutting criteria, have adverse effect on the performance of economic and social functions of the state, and thus on the quality of life of residents in terms of the protection of their life, health, safety, property, as well as the environment; b) Critical infrastructure sector (hereinafter referred to as the "sector") means part of the critical infrastructure which includes the elements; the sector may comprise one or more critical infrastructure sub-sectors (hereinafter referred to as the "subsector"); c) Critical infrastructure means a system, which is divided into sectors and elements Source: Slovak law No 45/2011
Spain	Critical Infrastructures are those strategic infrastructures (facilities, networks, systems and physical equipment, on which operation of essential services rest) which are indispensable, and where alternative solution is not possible, so that their disruption or destruction would seriously impact essential services. Source : CNPIC (2017) http://www.cnpic.es/en/Legislacion_Aplicable/Generico/index.html
Sweden	Those assets, systems or parts thereof located in the EU Member States which are essential for the maintenance of vital societal functions, health, safety, security, economic or social well-being of people, and the disruption or destruction of which would have a significant impact in a Member State as a result of the failure to maintain those functions. The term Critical Infrastructure (CI) refers to the activities, facilities, nodes, infrastructure and services that maintain Vital Societal Functions (VSF). Vital Societal Functions (VSF) is the term for the activities that maintain a given functionality. Each such function is included in one or more societal sectors Source: Swedish Civil Contingencies Agency, 2016; Action Plan for the Protection of Vital Societal Functions & Critical Infrastructure (2014)
Switzerland	Critical infrastructures are processes, systems and facilities that are essential for the functioning of the economy and the well-being of the population, respectively Source: OECD Survey on critical infrastructure (2017)
Turkey	Whole of networks, assets, systems and structures that would form serious impacts on safety, economy, health of citizens as a result of negative effect on conduct of environment, social order and public service in case it fails to fulfil its function partially or completely. Source: OECD Survey on critical infrastructure (2017)
United Kingdom	Those critical elements of infrastructure (namely assets, facilities, systems, networks or processes and the essential workers that operate and facilitate them), the loss or compromise of which could result in: a) Major detrimental impact on the availability, integrity or delivery of essential services – including those services whose integrity, if compromised, could result in significant loss of life or casualties – taking into account significant economic or social impacts; and/or b) Significant impact on national security, national defence, or the functioning of the state. Source: OECD Survey on critical infrastructure (2017)
United States	Critical infrastructure represents systems and assets, whether physical or virtual, so vital to the United States that the incapacity or destruction of such systems and assets would have a debilitating impact on security, national economic security, national public health or safety, or any combination of those matters. Source: The National Infrastructure Protection Plan 2013 Partnering for Critical Infrastructure Security and Resilience
United Nations	The physical structures, facilities, networks and other assets, which provide services that, are essential to the social and economic functioning of a community or society. Source: UNISDR Terminology on Disaster Risk Reduction https://www.unisdr.org/we/inform/terminology

Annex 3.C. List of critical sectors per OECD countries

	AUS	AUT	BEL	CAN	CHE	CHL	CZE	DEU	ESP	EST	FIN	FRA	GBR	GRC	IRL	ISL	ISR	ITA	KOR	LAT	LUX	MEX	NLD	NOR	NZL	POL	PRT	SVK	SVN	SWE	TUR	USA
Energy	•	•	•	•	•	•	•	•	•	•	•	•	•	•	•	•	•	•	•	•	•	•	•	•	•	•	•	•	•	•	•	•
Nuclear sector				•			•		•			•	•				•		•				•	•								•
ICT	•	•	•	•	•	•	•	•	•	•	•	•	•	•	•	•	•	•	•	•	•	•	•	•	•	•		•	•	•	•	•
Transportation	•	•	•	•	•	•	•	•	•		•	•	•	•	•	•	•	•	•	•	•	•	•	•	•	•	•	•	•	•	•	•
Water	•	•	•	•	•		•	•	•	•	•	•	•				•		•	•	•		•	•	•	•		•				•
Dams & flood defence	•					•	•					•			•	•		•	•	•		•	•	•					•		•	•
Food supply & dist.	•	•		•	•		•	•	•		•	•	•				•				•			•		•				•	•	•
Health	•	•	•	•	•	•	•	•	•	•	•	•	•				•		•	•	•			•		•		•		•	•	•
Finance & banking	•	•	•	•	•		•	•	•	•	•	•	•				•		•	•	•		•	•		•		•		•	•	•
Government		•		•	•		•	•	•			•	•				•		•	•	•			•		•				•		•
Public safety	•	•		•	•		•	•	•				•				•			•	•		•	•						•		•
Law enforcement		•				•		•				•	•				•			•	•		•	•								
Chemical industry	•	•			•				•		•	•	•				•			•	•		•	•		•		•				•
Space sector			•						•			•	•																			
Defence industry	•										•	•	•				•			•												•
Critical manufacturing				•							•	•					•							•							•	•
Other		•	•					•	•	•	•	•	•				•		•	•	•		•	•	•	•				•	•	•

Annex 3.D. List and descriptions of policy tools to strengthen critical infrastructures resilience

Policy tool	Description
Provision of hazards and threats information	Governments provide the results of national or infrastructure-specific hazard and threats assessments to owners and operators of critical infrastructure.
Voluntary information-sharing mechanisms or platforms	Governments encourage critical infrastructure owners and operators to share information relevant to the security and resilience of assets and systems amongst each other and with the government on a voluntary basis.
Mandatory information-sharing mechanisms or platforms	Laws and regulations require critical infrastructure operators to share information relevant to the security and resilience of assets and systems with the government.
Awareness raising activities and trainings	Awareness raising activities and trainings promote a risk culture within critical infrastructure. Trainings and exercises test the emergency management systems of critical infrastructure, and create familiarity with corresponding responsibilities during crises.
Resilience guidelines for critical infrastructure operators	Resilience guidelines outline steps and methods that operators of critical infrastructure should carry out to improve the resilience of their assets and systems at large. Such guidelines can be narrow in scope, providing e.g. only guidance for hazard assessments at operator level, or wide in scope, listing multiple tools and measures.
Fostering the development/use of professional standard	Development of professional standards for critical infrastructure resilience such as codes and benchmarks for capabilities and standards of operations.
Incentive mechanism to assess risks and vulnerabilities	Governments provide incentives that encourage operators of critical infrastructure to carry out hazard, risk and vulnerabilities assessments. Incentives could be the provision of technical support and guidance documents, or reward mechanisms, such as publicized reviews of meeting resiliency targets or certifications.
Incentive mechanisms for investing in resilience	Governments provide incentives that encourage operators of critical infrastructure to invest in critical infrastructure resilience include: subsidies, cost-benefit analysis, or government participating in insurance schemes.
Sectoral prescriptive regulations dedicated to CIP	Governments design regulations that specify operators of critical infrastructure to carry out certain This tool sets mandatory obligations for critical infrastructure to meet to ensure protection and resilience based on s77ectoral specificities.
Performance-based regulations on business continuity	Regulations that provide incentives for critical infrastructure operators to reach a targeted level of performance for maintaining services during disruptions.
Mandatory business continuity plans	Governments require operators of critical infrastructure to develop business continuity plans. Such plans feature prevention and preparedness measures (incl. contingency plans) that operators can rely on during hazardous events to ensure that business operations can keep running.
Inspections and performance assessments	Mandated inspectors check that operators of critical infrastructure have implemented the required resilience measures.
Fines for non-compliance with resilience requirements	In cases where inspections find that operators of critical infrastructure have not carried out the required resilience measures, the government issues fines (see incentive mechanisms).
Other types of penalties for non-compliance	Other types of penalties for non-compliance can include: revoking an operational license or temporary removal from service until requirements are met.

Ranking based on inspection / performance results	The government ranks and advertises the results of inspection/performances. Operators have an interest in doing well in such rankings, as maintaining their image and reputation is an important business success factor.
Reporting on operators resilience	Self-assessments on the resilience of operators of critical infrastructure and sharing the results with government and/or the wider public.
Sharing best practices	Using case-studies and results from events can indicate good practices for making critical infrastructure more resilient. Sharing best practices is an effective information tool to indicate how similar critical infrastructure owners and operators may address sectoral security issues, including relevant interdependencies on other sectors.
Public investments in infrastructure resilience	Government investments in resilience are applied to new public infrastructure in addition to ensuring that resilience gaps are being met where there are needs. Public financing for building resilient critical infrastructure systems can set standards for industry and demonstrate the value of these up-front investments in resilience.
Guidance for sub-national levels of government	Guidelines for sub-national level of government on awareness about critical infrastructure in their respective jurisdictions and close by that may pose transboundary risks, and how to strengthen resilience of these systems.
Mandatory insurance for critical infrastructure	Obligations set for critical infrastructure owners and operators to purchase insurance ex-ante a situation of shock or disruption of services.
Peer-reviews, monitoring and evaluation	Experts review and evaluate progress based on agreed upon evaluation criteria according sector-specific resilience guidelines... The outcome may identify potential gaps and provide suggestions for areas of improvement.

Annex 3.E. Country practices on critical infrastructure resilience identified in the OECD Toolkit on Risk Governance (TRIG)

Trusted Information Sharing Network for Critical Infrastructure in Australia

The Trusted Information Sharing Network (TISN) for Critical Infrastructure Resilience was established by the Australian Government in 2003, with the aim of assisting critical infrastructure organisations to better prevent, prepare, respond to and recover from disruptions and adverse events. The TISN provides national level forums for owners and operators of critical infrastructure to discuss critical infrastructure vulnerabilities with relevant government agencies and to work together in developing strategies and solutions to mitigate risk. Led by the Attorney-General's Department, and supported by a number of Australian Government agencies, the TISN now encompasses hundreds of members, including representatives from many of Australia's largest and best known companies, and state and territory governments. The TISN operates on an all-hazards basis. It comprises seven critical infrastructure Sector Groups (Energy, Water, Communications, Banking and Finance, Health, Transport, Food) and two Expert Advisory Groups. TISN members meet regularly within their sector groups in a secure, non-competitive environment to share vital information on risks and mitigation strategies, and to develop collective solutions to shared problems. In addition, there are regular meetings and exercises between groups, and with governments.

Rationale

Critical infrastructure delivers essential services such as food, water, healthcare, electricity, communications, transportation and banking. Without these services, Australia's social cohesion, economic prosperity and public safety are threatened. The Trusted Information Sharing Network responds to this by providing a forum for public and private stakeholders to cooperate towards critical infrastructure resilience.

Objectives

- Operate an effective business-government partnership with critical infrastructure owners and operators;
- Sharing information and techniques required to assess and mitigate risks to critical infrastructure;
- Building resilience capacity within organisations.

Results

- Since its creation, the TISN has influenced the national debate on critical infrastructure issues by partnering with key stakeholders to enable change;
- The TISN has fostered a cohesive approach to addressing shared threats and vulnerabilities and building resilience across critical infrastructure sectors;

- TISN initiatives include the development of shared frameworks, guides and planning documents, the preparation of large-scale exercises, and the organisation of workshops. These initiatives have contributed to enhance the resilience of critical infrastructure systems in Australia.

Lessons Learned

- There are major benefits to setting up platforms for information sharing among policy makers and owners and operators of critical infrastructure
- Business-government partnerships are key to encourage the private sector to address mutual interests, such as business continuity and resilience.
- There are major benefits to setting up platforms for information sharing among policy makers and owners and operators of critical infrastructure.
- Business-government partnerships are key to encourage the private sector to address mutual interests, such as business continuity and resilience.

Source:https://www.oecd.org/governance/toolkit-on-risk-governance/goodpractices/page/trustedinformationsharingnetworkforcriticalinfrastructureinaustralia.htm

Integrated approach for Critical Infrastructure Protection in the Netherlands

A new integrated approach for critical infrastructure protection was established in May 2015 as part of the National Safety and Security Strategy, developed by the Dutch Ministry for Security and Justice. The approach contains three steps. First, the approach identifies what is critical infrastructure, based on economic, physical and social impact criteria. Criteria were developed based on the National Risk Assessment process. The degree of criticality depends upon the consequences of a failure of the critical sectors identified. A distinction is made between category A where disruptions can have large impacts and cascading effects and category B where impacts can be lower, in order to reflect the diversity within critical infrastructure and to set priorities. Secondly, a vulnerability assessment provides insight into the most important risks, threats, vulnerabilities and degree of resilience of this infrastructure. The third step of the approach is to make agreements on maintaining or, where needed, increasing the resilience of the vital infrastructure. This enables a customized approach for resilience enhancement, based on risks, threats and vulnerabilities. In addition, critical infrastructure will be incorporated into the national crisis management structures.

Rationale

Guaranteeing the continuity of critical infrastructure is of common interest to both infrastructures operators (usually private) and to society in the Netherlands. Critical infrastructure includes products, services and underlying processes which, should they fail, could cause large-scale social disruption. That is why the government and critical organisations in the Netherlands cooperate in protecting this infrastructure. An integrated approach is required, due to the number of parties, networks and levels involved. This is a dynamic and complex domain due to technological developments and interconnectedness of critical processes. Society has become more dependent on critical infrastructure while the failure of such infrastructure has become less accepted in society. Infrastructure has become more dependent and has become more vulnerable to (deliberate) cyber incidents. Moreover, the interconnectedness of critical processes makes it difficult to predict cascade effects. Cascading effects caused by failing processes leads to higher impact on society.

Objectives

- Resilient critical infrastructure
- Impacted based identification of critical infrastructure
- Understanding of risk, threats and vulnerabilities
- Development of customized agreements

Results

- Impact based identification methodology
- From sectorial approach to a process approach
- Identification of critical infrastructure at the national level
- national level prioritised list of critical infrastructure
- Tailor made agreements per critical process
- Monitoring and evaluation methodology

Lessons Learned

- Fostering an all-hazard approach is a good way to engage with private operators as they may be particularly interested in one specific threat without having the largest view on risks
- Having clear and transparent criteria well established for the identification of critical infrastructure helps engaging the different stakeholders.
- It requires a political decision what impact criteria are regarded as disruptive. There is a risk that changes in societal preferences may lead to changes in the thresholds, which would ask for a reassessment of critical infrastructure.
- Developing partnerships with private operators requires developing trust across the public and the private sector and a common understanding of the challenges, which develops over the long-term.

Source:https://www.oecd.org/governance/toolkit-on-risk-governance/goodpractices/page/integratedapproachforcriticalinfrastructureprotectioninthenetherlands.htm

National Strategy for Critical Infrastructure Protection in Germany

The German National Strategy for Critical Infrastructure Protection summarizes the Federal Administration's aims and objectives and its political-strategic approach to actively address matters of critical infrastructure protection (CIP). The strategy is guided by the principle of joint action by the state, society, and business and industry. The state co-operates with other public and private actors in developing analyses and protection concepts. The Strategy first defines critical infrastructure, as organizational and physical structures and facilities of such vital importance to a nation's society and economy that their failure or degradation would result in sustained supply shortages, significant disruption of public safety and security, or other dramatic consequences. It also identifies main threats, risks and vulnerabilities of critical infrastructure systems in Germany. Its guiding principle is that the responsibility for the security, reliability and availability of such infrastructure is a shared-responsibility. The Strategy takes stock of existing measures, and suggests a way forward to structure the different initiatives and further improve the protection of critical infrastructure systems. It develops guidelines in the prevention, response and sustainability areas, based on three pillars: (1) Preventing and mitigating loss of services

(2) Promoting back-up systems (redundancies) and emergency capacity (3) Enhancing self-protection capabilities. Developments are currently ongoing with regard to the protection of critical infrastructures in Germany

Rationale

Infrastructure in general and critical infrastructure in particular are vital to the functioning and well-being of modern and efficient societies. Germany is among the leading industrial and technology-oriented nations. Germany is also an important location for business activities and industry. Ensuring the country's competitiveness in a globalized economic and technological setting is highly dependent on the availability of high-performance and well-functioning infrastructure. Therefore, ensuring the protection of this infrastructure is a key function of security-related preparedness measures taken by industry and government agencies, and is a central issue of the country's security policy.

Objectives

- Guiding the Federal Government but also the Länder, municipalities and enterprises in their critical infrastructure protection efforts.
- Promote critical infrastructure resilience in a coordinated manner
- Strengthen public safety and security
- Foster joint action performed by the Government, companies and/or operations and the civil society for critical infrastructure protection

Results

- Implementation of work packages within the Federation, Lander and local governments involving (1) the definition of general protection targets, (2) an analysis of threats, vulnerabilities and management capabilities, (3) the assessment of threats, (4) the specification of protection targets, taking into account existing protective measures; analysis of existing regulations and, where applicable, identification of additional measures contributing to goal attainment; and where required, legislation.
- Development of programmes and Plans (such as the National Plan for Information Infrastructure Protection), specific recommendations for action (such as the National Baseline Protection Concept, the Risk and Crisis Management Guide for Critical Infrastructure Operations, and standards, norms and regulations (such as BSI Information Security Standards, or the regulations of the German Gas and Water Supply Association on risk management in the field of drinking water supply).

Lessons Learned

- Preserving critical infrastructure protection is of growing importance, particularly in the context of increasingly interdependent economies.
- Co-operations and partnerships in the area of critical infrastructure both with authorities and in particular with private service providers is vital to guarantee successful work.
- The aim of a critical infrastructure strategy should not be absolute protection, but implementing measures that foster resilience.
- Cross-sectoral cooperation and coordination is key to achieving resilience of critical infrastructure.

Source:https://www.oecd.org/governance/toolkit-on-risk-governance/goodpractices/page/nationalstrategyforcriticalinfrastructureprotectioningermany.htm

Swiss Basic Strategy for Critical Infrastructure Protection

The Swiss National Strategy for the Protection of Critical Infrastructure was established in 2012, drawing upon the "Basic Strategy for Critical Infrastructure Protection" (2009). The overarching goal of the Strategy is to improve the resilience of Switzerland's critical infrastructures. The Strategy outlines strategic goals as well as key principles, and describes the measures to be taken in the area of critical infrastructure. These measures include the improvement of the overall critical infrastructure resiliency, and the enhancement of the general framework for cross-sectoral collaboration. The Strategy covers the definition of comprehensive protection approaches, the identification and compilation of critical infrastructure elements and objects in a classified inventory, the establishment of cross-sectoral, public-private platforms, and information sharing on risks, notably risk assessment and warning systems, among stakeholders. The Strategy also addresses federal support to handle disruptions to critical infrastructure, if the operators' and substate actors' resources are overwhelmed. It establishes a permanent process to improve the resilience of critical infrastructure systems by facilitating a coordinated approach among the relevant CI operators as well as specialised and regulatory agencies. Ten sectors are considered critical at the national level, including energy, transport, information and communication technologies, financial services, public administration, public health, public safety, and transport. They are subdivided into 28 subsectors like natural gas supply, oil supply and power supply in the sector energy supply.

Rationale

Switzerland is highly dependent on the continuous operation of critical infrastructures that ensure the supply of vital goods and services. Disruptions may have rapid repercussions for the population and the basis of its livelihood, and can affect other critical infrastructure through cascading effects. In the different critical sector, protection measures are already implemented on an individual basis. However, the lack of cross-sectoral coordination among critical infrastructure stakeholders and the need to promote a consolidated approach at the national level created the need for an integrated national strategy.

Objectives

- Contributing to maintain the operability of critical infrastructure systems,
- Identifying critical infrastructure systems to be protected,
- Facilitating risk analysis procedures,
- Initiating cross-sectoral collaboration by setting up coordination and information sharing platforms.

Results

- Classified critical infrastructure inventory
- Created a critical infrastructure guideline
- Conducted sub-sectoral risk and vulnerability assessments
- Established supporting tools (e.g. methodology, scenarios, etc.)

Lessons Learned

- Critical infrastructure protection is becoming more and more important today, in particular in major cities and small interdependent countries such as Switzerland.
- The aim of a critical infrastructure strategy should not be absolute protection, but implementing measures to foster resilience.
- Cross-sectoral cooperation and coordination is key.
- Cross-country cooperation should be encouraged in an increasingly globalised world.

Source:https://www.oecd.org/governance/toolkit-on-risk-governance/goodpractices/page/swissbasicstrategyforcriticalinfrastructureprotection.htm

Public Private Partnerships for Critical Infrastructures Resilience in Finland

The National Emergency Supply Agency (NESA), created in 1993, is tasked with planning, developing and maintaining the security of supply in Finland. While its historic role of maintaining reserve stockpiles to protect the livelihoods of the population as well as the functioning of the economy remains part of its strategic tasks, NESA is more and more active in mainstreaming business continuity and resilience in various sectors of the economy through public-private partnerships. NESA has established a network of thematic clusters where key stakeholders of critical sectors, such as: food supply, energy, transportation, health or industry, develop partnerships in order to assess vulnerability and performance and plan for resilience. NESA also proposes dedicated tools, such as information systems, storage and transport facilities to support business continuity on these domains. NESA also finances specific activities related to business continuity and critical infrastructure protection. The agency prepares annual reports that evaluate the performance of companies in the critical sectors including ranking and specific recommendations

Rationale

Finland faces specific vulnerabilities regarding the disruption of supply chains and critical infrastructures which constitute a major challenge. Harsh winter conditions, high dependence on sea transportation and international markets, interdependencies and the complexity of critical networks are among the key challenges to security of supplies in Finland. Consequently, Finland has invested significant efforts to secure supplies and maintain continuity of services. This is a primary concern of its Security Strategy for Society, in which the functioning of the economy and the infrastructure is one of the seven vital functions of Finnish society. NESA contributes to the implementation of the functioning of society in times of crisis by keeping reserve stockpiles but also by guiding critical infrastructure providers the necessary knowledge about preparedness and continuity planning.

Objectives

- Securing supplies to ensure the continuity of the economic activities and the functioning of critical infrastructure in cases of serious disturbances and exceptional circumstances;
- Setting-up private-public partnerships as the primary method for securing supply and developing business continuity;

- Implementing technical and financial measures to support the development of business continuity efforts across society production of goods and services necessary in exceptional conditions.

Results

- Increased public-private partnerships with companies in critical sectors (now more than 1000) which all yielded a business continuity plan specific to their activities and sector;
- Established 7 thematic clusters and dedicated pools to discuss and implement sector-specific supply security and business continuity policies;
- Developed continuity-management tools designed to support organizations in their continuity management efforts.

Lessons Learned

- Public bodies within countries should not take full responsibility to maintain the continuity of services, but also the private sector should invest some efforts into preparedness in order to achieve a whole-of-society approach of risk prevention
- Incentivizing private sector's efforts in business continuity is essential to facilitate their involvement in these efforts. Evaluating the performance of individual companies is a complementary and efficient way to stir progress.
- As security of supplies and continuity of critical infrastructures is market-dependent, specific attention to issues related to fair competition, non-discrimination and equal treatment are fundamental when designing policies

Source:https://www.oecd.org/governance/toolkit-on-risk-governance/goodpractices/page/publicprivatepartnershipsforcriticalinfrastructuresresilienceinfinland.htm

National Critical Infrastructure Protection Programme in Poland

The Polish National Critical Infrastructure Protection Programme (NCIPP) was adopted in March 2013 by the Polish Council of Ministers, with the main objective of ensuring the protection of critical infrastructure systems. The NCIPP defines the vision and the objectives behind critical infrastructure protection processes and covers all the phases of the risk management cycle: it aims not only to ensure critical infrastructure's protection against threats (prevention), but also to contribute to reduce the impact and length of the potential damages (preparedness and response). The NCIPP addresses the following infrastructure systems: energy, communication, ICTs, financial, food supply, water supply, health protection, transportation, rescue, public administration and the production, storage and use of chemical and radioactive substances. The NCIPP describes the cooperation to be set between individuals, and sets out roles and responsibilities for each stakeholder. The NCIPP pays particular attention to building partnerships between stakeholders. Information and knowledge sharing between all levels of the administration as well as between the public and the private sector are key in protecting infrastructure systems. The NCIPP also identifies a number of good practices and recommendations to ensure the smooth functioning of critical infrastructure, in several areas such as technical protection, IT/OT protection, legal protection, business continuity/recovery plans. The good practices and recommendations have been broadened, especially in the area of IT/OT protection. In November 2015, the NCIPP has been updated. It now includes new priorities and tasks for the 2015-2017 period

Rationale

Critical infrastructure is key to the smooth functioning of the public and private sectors. Protecting critical infrastructure in Poland is therefore essential for the smooth functioning of the economic system; Critical infrastructure resilience is also a priority as it can negatively impact the lives of the Polish citizens.

Objectives

- Increase the resilience of critical infrastructure systems in Poland;
- Raise awareness about the importance of critical infrastructure and enhance risk assessment frameworks;
- Allow coordinated and risk-based partnerships for the protection of critical infrastructure

Results

- Three meetings of the National Forum for Infrastructure Protection have been organised, gathering representatives from the private sector and the administration to exchange on the resilience of critical infrastructure in Poland.
- Four textbooks were developed: on verifying the authenticity of the documents, on explosive threats to critical infrastructure, on applying biometrics to critical infrastructure, and on technical protection of critical infrastructure systems
- Over 800 individuals were trained in the fields covered by these textbooks.

Lessons Learned

- People are the most valuable resource for protecting critical infrastructure. Their knowledge, experience and commitment are key to achieve determined goals.
- A strategy related to risk management must encompass clear objectives and action plans, and precisely define the roles of each stakeholder.
- Broad-based partnerships and information sharing are essential to promote critical infrastructure protection.

Source:https://www.oecd.org/governance/toolkit-on-risk-governance/goodpractices/page/nationalcriticalinfrastructureprotectionprogrammeinpoland.htm

Canada's National Strategy for Critical Infrastructure

The National Strategy for Critical Infrastructure sets the direction for enhancing the resilience of Canada's critical infrastructure against current and emerging hazards. The Strategy presents a collaborative approach to strengthening the resilience of critical infrastructure, by ensuring that federal, provincial and territorial critical infrastructure activities are complementary and respect the laws of each jurisdiction. It outlines mechanisms for enhanced information sharing and information protection, and identifies the importance of a risk management approach to strengthen the resilience of critical infrastructure in Canada. Enhancing the resilience of critical infrastructure can be achieved through the appropriate combination of security measures to address intentional and accidental incidents, business continuity practices to deal with disruptions and ensure the continuation of essential services. It also addresses the importance of emergency management planning to ensure adequate response procedures are in place to deal with unforeseen disruptions and natural disasters.. At the national level, the Strategy classifies critical infrastructure within the 10 following sectors: energy and utilities, finance, food, transportation, government, information and communication technology, health, safety, water, manufacturing

Rationale

As the risks to critical infrastructure cut across jurisdictions and sectors, the Strategy provides a comprehensive and collaborative federal, provincial and territorial approach to enhancing the resilience of critical infrastructure. This common approach enables partners to respond collectively to risks and target resources to the most vulnerable areas of critical infrastructure.

Objectives

- Building partnerships at all levels of government, and with the private sector;
- Implementing an all-hazards risk management approach;
- Advancing the timely sharing of information among partners

Results

The National Strategy was accompanied by an Action Plan for Critical Infrastructure (2010), which set out action items for each of the three strategic objectives. A summary of progress achieved under the original Action Plan is contained in the renewed Action Plan for Critical Infrastructure (2014-2017). The next phase of the Action Plan involves taking additional steps for each of the three strategic objectives outlined in the National Strategy, building on what was already achieved under the original Action Plan (2010), with an emphasis on tangible risk management activities

Lessons Learned

- Critical infrastructure protection is becoming more and more important today, in particular in the context of increasingly interdependent economies.
- The aim of a critical infrastructure strategy should not be absolute protection, but implementing measures that foster resilience.
- Cross-sectoral cooperation and coordination is key.

Source:https://www.oecd.org/governance/toolkit-on-risk-governance/goodpractices/page/canadasnationalstrategyforcriticalinfrastructure.htm

US Critical Infrastructure Protection and Resilience Toolkit

The U.S. Department of Homeland Security created the Critical Infrastructure Protection and Resilience Toolkit for owners and operators of critical infrastructure at the local and regional levels to enhance their ability to prepare for, protect against, respond to, and recover from the full range of 21st-century hazards and threats. The toolkit is designed to help critical infrastructure owners and operators incorporate key concepts of the US National Infrastructure Protection Plan (NIPP) into their day-to-day activities. The toolkit includes: A brief video that highlights the role of local and regional communities and the private sector in national infrastructure protection efforts. An exercise planning resource that provides simple tools to help owners and operators plan a discussion-based “table top” exercise to evaluate infrastructure protection and resilience. Frequently asked questions about the role of owners and operators in critical infrastructure protection and resilience. Links to additional online reference materials and training resources related to infrastructure protection and resilience. Information on critical infrastructure protection partnerships and information sharing.

Rationale

As critical infrastructure systems, essential health services must remain available to communities and individuals during and immediately following extreme weather events, even during extended utility outages and transportation infrastructure disturbances. Resilient health care organizations must anticipate extreme weather risks and transcend limitations of regional public policy, local development vulnerabilities, and community infrastructure challenges as they site, construct, and retrofit health care facilities. The disruptions and losses incurred by the U.S. health care sector following recent extreme weather events demonstrate the need for specific guidance on ways to manage the new and evolving hazards presented by climate change. During Super Storm Sandy in New York, for example, several hospitals had to be evacuated because their back-up electricity generators were located in the basement and ended up being flooded, or because there was no plan to fuel them during a longer period than 24 h. In addition some of their most expensive equipment, such as X-Rays were also in the hospital's basement and contributed to large losses in the sector. These events have also provided opportunities to learn from past disasters so that health care facilities, and the communities they serve, can be more resilient in the future. For these reasons, the Department of Health and Human Services has developed the Sustainable and Climate Resilient Health Care Facilities Toolkit to support building resilience in the health care sector.

Objectives

- Share best practices for health care providers, design professionals, policy makers, and others to promote continuity of care before, during, and after extreme weather events.
- Assess the current status of health care infrastructure to extreme weather risks, and policy options that can be adopted to improve climate readiness.
- Assist organizations engaged in health care facility climate resilience to improve their resilience to extreme weather events.

Results

- The Toolkit contains a set of checklists for each of the five elements of climate resilience. These checklists can assist health care organizations in assessing climate-related infrastructure and care-delivery vulnerabilities at both a system and facility level and evaluating the results of their resiliency policies.
- The Climate Resilience Toolkit also includes tools and processes for converting the results of the checklist exercise into a practical plan for improved resilience, and will facilitate identification of policies to implement based on the assessment provided by the checklist.

Lessons Learned

- Sectorial plans that provide sector-specific guidance on risk preparedness and resiliency are useful to ensure the relevance and the appropriation of policy options.

Source:https://www.oecd.org/governance/toolkit-on-risk-governance/goodpractices/page/uscriticalinfrastructureprotectionandresiliencetoolkit.htm

UK Centre for the Protection of National Infrastructure (CPNI)

The Centre for the Protection of National Infrastructure (CPNI) protects national security by providing advice to the UK national infrastructure organisations, covering physical, personnel and cyber security. To achieve protective security in the national infrastructure sectors, the CPNI supports vulnerability reduction efforts to terrorism and other threats, keeping the UK's essential services (delivered by communications, emergency services, energy, finance, food, government, health, transport and water sectors) safer. Without these services, the UK could suffer serious consequences, including severe economic damage, grave social disruption, or even large scale loss of life. CPNI advice primarily targets critical national infrastructure organisations, which are crucial to the continued delivery of essential services to the UK. CPNI works both with private and public sector partners. Key partners include as the National Technical Authority for Information Assurance (CESG) and the police - National Counter Terrorism Security Office (NaCTSO) and the Counter Terrorism Security Advisor (CTSA) network, as well as critical national infrastructure businesses and organisations. CPNI was formed on 1 February 2007 from the merger of the National Infrastructure Security Co-ordination Centre (NISCC) and the National Security Advice Centre (NSAC). NISCC used to provide advice to companies operating in critical national infrastructure, while NSAC was a unit within MI5 that provided security advice to other parts of the UK government.

Rationale

National critical infrastructure is recognized as "'those critical elements of infrastructure" (namely assets, facilities, systems, networks or processes and the essential workers that operate and facilitate them), the loss or compromise of which could result in: a) major detrimental impact on the availability, integrity or delivery of essential services – including those services, whose integrity, if compromised, could result in significant loss of life or casualties – taking into account significant economic or social impacts; and/or b) significant impact on national security, national defence, or the functioning of the state. Achieving protective security, i.e. 'putting in place, or building into design, security measures or protocols such that threats may be deterred, detected, or the consequences of an attack minimized', in critical infrastructure is therefore crucial to prevent severe economic damage, social disruption or large scale loss of lives.

Objectives

- Support vulnerability reduction efforts to terrorism and other threats in the UK's critical infrastructure
- Address major threats as identified in the UK National Security Strategy, i.e. espionage, terrorism, cyber and other threats
- Provide security advice and security planning services to critical infrastructure operators
- Protect national security

Results

In recent years, the CPNI has issued periodic warnings about increasing levels of cybercrime. Securing digital systems, including open wireless access points, implementing strong firewalls and encrypting communications are all important priorities, analogous to securing physical property and facilities.

Lessons Learned

Offering centralized advice to critical national infrastructure organisations on vulnerability and security aspects, is an essential component of raising awareness on the matter. In this way guidance helps infrastructure make better informed decisions and respond to early warning signs.

Source:https://www.oecd.org/governance/toolkit-on-risk-governance/goodpractices/page/centrefortheprotectionofnationalinfrastructurecpni.htm

4. Critical infrastructure resilience case-study: Electricity transmission and distribution in Finland

The case-study of Finland's electricity transmission and distribution system in this chapter illustrates how governments can set-up an effective governance model that fosters investments in infrastructure resilience. Finland has been nurturing a cooperative framework to strengthen critical infrastructure resilience that stresses public private cooperation, information sharing and consensus building on policy design and objective setting. With ambitious resilience targets, this governance model has shown great results in its first years of implementation. Nevertheless, new challenges have emerged including how to address the implications in terms of costs for customers, the difference between larger and smaller operators' capacities, as well as the implications of digitalisation and climate change.

Introduction

The electricity transmission and distribution network is designated as critical infrastructure services in Finland and disruptions of energy supply is considered among the most critical national risks. The supply of electricity is vital for functioning of society and the economy, especially given the high degree of dependencies of many other critical sectors upon power supply (e.g. telecommunications, water, transport). In Finland, harsh climate conditions, a dispersed population and ageing infrastructure expose the electricity network to a range of risks. On top of weather-related hazards, technological accidents, hybrid threats, and cyber-attacks call for greater attention with the potential vulnerabilities linked to technological developments in the sector, characterized by increased automation, digitalization, deployment of smart grids and interdependencies with ICTs.

Finland has set itself the objective of being the safest society in Europe. Reaching national resilience goals necessitates strengthening the resilience of national critical infrastructure and in particular the electricity network. Experiences with extreme weather in Finland illustrate the large-scale consequences of electricity disruptions. In December 2011 the severe windstorm Tapani left over 500,000 people without electricity, from several hours up to 3 weeks – impacting the livelihood of communities, telecommunication and water systems, business closures and more. Repair costs of the electricity network were estimated to reach 102.5 million euros, and operators paid 71 million euros of compensation to customers. Following the event, public discontent on the extensive interruptions led to political discussions on the urgent need to revamp preparedness measures in the electricity network. In 2013 regulations in the Electricity Market Act were updated and new resilience targets set up to reach by 31.12.2028. Additional modifications were made to limited outage times, with compensation schemes and penalties for distribution operators.

This case study discusses the governance issues related to strengthening the resilience of the electricity transmission and distribution network in Finland. Along with the 2028 resilience targets, Finland has been cultivating a cooperative framework to strengthening critical infrastructure resilience that stresses public private cooperation, information sharing and consensus building on policy design and objective setting. The governance approach is steered by sector-specific security of supply policies and a comprehensive national strategy that involves multi-stakeholder participations and coordination. This approach involves a mix of policy instruments to incentivise investments in resilience, both regulatory and voluntary. The case-study illustrates these good practices in Finland, and also presents some challenges to overcome and to continue improving the resilience of electricity transmission and distribution in a dynamic risk landscape.

Electricity transmission and distribution network as critical infrastructure in Finland

Power supply is a priority in Finland

Energy production, transmission and distribution networks are deemed critical infrastructure services in Finland, and resilience against disruptions are considered as one of the highest priorities. The 2013 Government decision on the security of supply goals lists disturbances in the electricity grid as the first major threat to the Finnish society's capability to function properly (Ministry of Employment and the Economy, 2013). The 2015 National Risk Assessment further highlights the criticality of power supply for the functioning of society and the economy, and provides a list of scenarios of serious disruptions and their potential impacts (Ministry of Interior, 2016). The National Risk

Assessment informs the Security Strategy for Society (2017), which presents reliable power supply as a basic requirement for all vital areas of society: its interruption may endanger other critical functions and affect the well-being of the population.

Finnish electricity transmission and distribution system

The concentration of power production, the dependency on electricity imports during peak periods, as well as Finland's vast territory and dispersed rural population, shapes the Finnish electricity transmission and distribution network. Power generation in Finland currently has a production capacity of 12 000 MW, generated by 150 companies in 400 production plants. While biomass, peat and hydropower electricity generation is spread out throughout the Finnish territory, nuclear and natural gas are concentrated in the southern part. The concentration of energy production is expected to increase in the south once the new nuclear reactor Olkiluoto 3 becomes operational, complementing the four existing ones in Loviisa and Olkiluoto. With an estimated peak demand exceeding 15 000 MW during the winter, Finland currently imports around 20% of its electricity, mostly from Sweden and Estonia through the Nordic electricity market pool, and also from Russia (Energy Authority, 2017).

The vast electricity transmission and distribution network is operated by a diversity of operators, with different levels of operational and financial capacities. As per European Union directives, the network is composed of one nation-wide transmission grid and a series of local monopolies for distribution. The state-controlled Transmission System Operator (TSO) Fingrid operates the main grid composed of around 14 400 km of high-voltage overhead lines and 113 sub-stations. It ensures a balance between electricity supply and demand, and manages cross-border inter-connections with Sweden (2 undersea and 2 overhead lines), Baltic countries and Russia. Medium and lower voltage regional and distribution networks cover 140 000 km (80% as overhead lines) and 240 000 km (60% as overhead cables) respectively. They are under the responsibility of 77 distribution system operators (DSO). A few among them operate the majority of the market and their ownership is a patchwork between public and private. For example, the Helsinki DSO Helen Sähköverkko is 100% owned by Helsinki city, the largest DSO Caruna is owned by a combination of private investors and pensions funds, and many small DSO in rural areas are owned by local municipalities. This makes DSOs very diverse in their capacities to invest in and maintain distribution networks and services.

As in many OECD countries, the Finnish electricity market is undergoing major changes driven by innovation and climate change policies. Megatrends such as the phasing out of coals by 2029, the growing share of renewable energy with intermittent production, the deployment of smart grids and automated control systems are leading to increased flexibility between supply and demand, as well as dependencies on information systems. These changes raise questions on how these evolutions will affect security of electricity supply and how TSO and DSOs will need to adapt.

Main risks and vulnerabilities of the Finnish electricity transmission and distribution system

Before 2010, the Finnish transmission and distribution system had extremely high reliability rates, but major storms put into question its resilience to climate-related risks, especially concerning distribution networks. Harsh climate conditions and long distances of the electricity network to a dispersed population across Finland makes power outages a critical risk with severe potential impacts (Forssen, 2016). In the 2015 National Risk

Assessment, the scenario of a large-scale winter storm is considered as the most probable serious regional event with the largest impact, notably due to electricity disruptions it can create. Large storms in 2010 and 2011 toppled trees onto overhead lines, which pass through the large forest areas of the country and are difficult to access for quick repair (Kufeoglu and Lehtonen, 2014). These events led to major socio-economic impacts in many sectors across the nation (Box 4.1). Regular snowstorms are also known to accumulate snow on overhead lines or on trees that can bend and break circuits or damage protective equipment.

The effects of climate change on hazard patterns and their potential consequences on risks to electricity transmission and distribution networks should also be carefully considered. The large-scale 2018 summer fires affecting neighbouring Sweden raised concerns that rising temperatures could lead to more frequent forest fires across Scandinavia, with potential implications on electricity networks. Sea level rise and coastal floods are another risk in Finland, particularly along the south-western coast and greater Helsinki area, where population density is the highest and flooded sub-stations could disrupt distribution. Although unrelated to climate change, the Finnish National Risk Assessment also mentions the specific risk of a 100-year return period solar storm and its repercussions on electricity systems.

Box 4.1. The Tapani windstorm in 2011

The December 2011 Dagmar cyclone, locally known as the Tapani storm, demonstrated how disruptive and damaging such extreme weather event can be on the electricity network. While an earlier storm in the 2010 summer, leaving 400 000 people without electricity, was a significant warning, Tapani's consequences were much more severe, as it happened in winter. With two consecutive waves of strong wind gusts affecting most of the western shore of Finland on the 26th and the 27th of December, the Tapani storm caused the largest disruption to society that Finland had experienced in years. 570 000 people were affected by electricity disruption, representing one of six households in the country, some of them for more than 15 days, due to the difficulty to restore services. Strong winds and falling trees caused more than 60 000 faults in the grid and interruptions of electricity supply had major cascading impacts, including on Fingrid's high-voltage transmission network. Heating systems, hospitals, water distribution and wastewater treatment plants were significantly affected, and the interruption of unpowered telecommunication services caused further repercussions: remote access connections to electricity substations were lost, Finnish authorities communication network broke down, and the electricity service restoration took a longer period. While estimates of all these indirect damages are not available, the storm incurred repair costs of up to 102.5 million euros for electricity operators, 120 million euros in forest damage and operators paid compensation of 71 million euros to their customers. This extreme weather disaster was a turning point for Finland to rethink security of supply policy in the electricity sector.

Source: (Kufeoglu and Lehtonen, 2014)

In addition to natural hazards, technical faults or accidents, interdependencies, and cyber threats or other security risks are key issues for an all-hazards and threats approach to the resilience of Finnish electricity transmission and distribution systems. On the 18 July 2018 a fire in a current transformer at the Olkiluoto substation burned protection cables (Fingrid, 2018). As a result, two nuclear power plants were shut down and taken off-grid, which posed a serious supply shock requiring the activation of energy reserves. It highlighted the potential domino effect of these types of accidents and need for preparedness planning. A similar situation during the winter consumption peak may have had much worse consequences on the main grid. Finland's reliance on imports from neighbouring countries, which can be affected by similar hazards from cold frost to winter storm, poses another major risk, in case of multiple failures affecting Nordic countries at the same time. Finally, interdependencies with other critical sectors and specifically with ICT networks is a key issue to reflect upon, as the electricity network operations are moving towards increased automation and digitalisation (Pantelli and Mancarella, 2017). This could create new vulnerabilities to cyber-attacks that authorities and operators alike should take seriously, especially in the context of increasing concerns of hybrid threats in Europe.

Governance of electricity transmission and distribution resilience

Finland has a well-established critical infrastructure policy

In this dynamic risk landscape, where interdependencies and interconnectedness of systems create the potential for damaging consequences of failures, Finland has been pioneering resilience of critical infrastructure in its risk management policy for a decade. With the ambitious goal to be the safest country in Europe, Finland's strategic framework for risk governance aligns well with the OECD Recommendation on the Governance of Critical Risks (OECD, 2014). The National Risk Assessment supports the whole-of-government Security Strategy for Society that puts vital functions for society at its core since 2010. With a focus on the resilience of the flow of services vital for functioning of society and government, this strategy fed into the 2013 Government Decision on the Security of Supply Goals. This policy document, first adopted in 1988 and revised around every 5-7 years ever since, defines the following resilience objectives: the continuity of economic activities and the functioning of critical infrastructure in the case of severe disruptions and emergencies. It also lists the critical infrastructure services of the country as follows: energy, data communication systems, financial services, transport and logistics, water supply, construction and maintenance, and waste management.

Finland's strategic approach assigns leadership to sectoral ministries for critical infrastructure resilience and emphasizes a collaborative framework leveraging on public private cooperation. The Security of Supply strategy harmonizes national preparedness principles across administrative branches by outlining clear roles and responsibilities across the whole-of-government, including at the local level (Ministry of Employment and the Economy, 2013). By highlighting the principles of cooperation with the private sector and coordination with international partners, this comprehensive strategy stresses the importance of partnerships and well-functioning markets and regulations for critical infrastructure resilience.

To support the implementation of critical infrastructure resilience policies, the National Emergency Supply Organisation (NESO) is the cornerstone for public and private cooperation, which allows building a shared vision of critical risks and resilience. NESO brings together industry and government in sector-specific pools, to develop a common understanding of critical infrastructure risks and vulnerabilities and discuss practical preparedness measures and business continuity planning. The National Emergency Supply Agency (NESA) under the Ministry of Economic Affairs and Employment is tasked to conduct risk analysis, coordinate information-sharing, foster public private cooperation, and mainstream security of supply policies in critical sectors. With more than a thousand companies engaged in the pooling system (Figure 4.1), NESO is considered as a well-functioning governance mechanism for critical infrastructure resilience by its participating stakeholders.

Figure 4.1. NESA pooling system: public private cooperation model

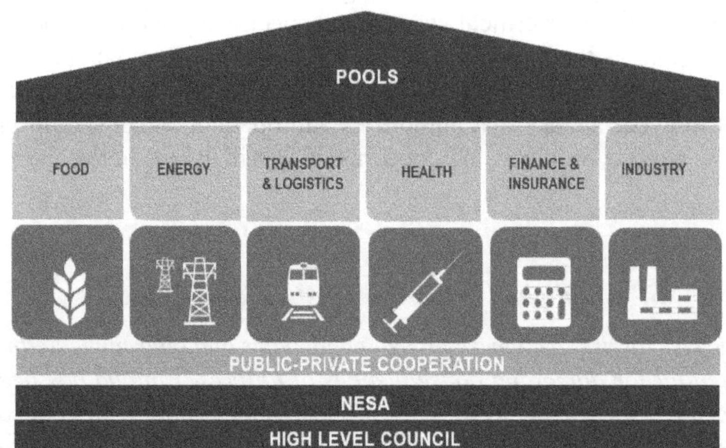

Electricity market regulations are also a key tool used in Finland to foster resilience

Finland's electricity market regulations have since a long time been paying close attention to the resilience of the transmission and distribution networks. As in most countries, the energy sector in Finland has a long history of regulation to ensure quality and reliability of services, containing security standards and measures to keep reasonable prices for customers. The 2003 Electricity Market Act set the regulatory framework for the energy sector and established outage time limits with variable penalties in the form of compensations to consumers commensurate to pre-set outages times above 12 hours of disruption (Ministry of Economic Affairs and Employment, 2013). This scaled approach was quite innovative at that time and complemented well other price incentives for distribution companies to increase the resilience of their networks, based on reliability and quality levels.

This sophisticated approach proved insufficient to avoid large-scale electricity supply disruptions during the 2010 and 2011 storms, which led the Ministry of Economic Affairs and Employment to revise regulations and strengthen incentivises for resilience investments. The 2013 revision of the Electricity Market Act adjusted the above-mentioned scheme, setting higher compensations paid by distribution operators to their customers in case of longer outage time. These compensations can now reach up to 200% of the yearly average electricity fee - up to a maximum of 2000 euros - when the disruption exceeds 12 days, compared to the previous 100% compensation rate above 5 days of outage time. While this regulation applies to all disruptions, the revised Act also sets compulsory resilience targets for weather hazards that operators should comply with by the end of 2028. It specifies that the longest acceptable interruption time will be of 6 hours in urban areas and 36 hours in rural areas. As the sector regulator, the Energy Authority assesses compliance of DSOs to intermediary objectives provided in approved investment plans that they are required to submit every two years (Figure 4.2). The regulation is grounded on an incentive mechanism, including quality and security of supply incentives. The former encourages DSO's to reach higher than minimum level of security of supply on account of outage costs, and the latter to meet regulatory criteria using cost-effective measures, and continue regular investments in maintenance and contingency. In addition, the 2013 Act makes business continuity plans mandatory for operators. The adoption of the new legislation required that all DSO's reapply for a license of operation in 2013, and these utilities now have a clear plan of action to boost investments in resilience and strengthen their preparedness efforts.

Figure 4.2. Intermediary objectives towards reaching 2018 resilience targets

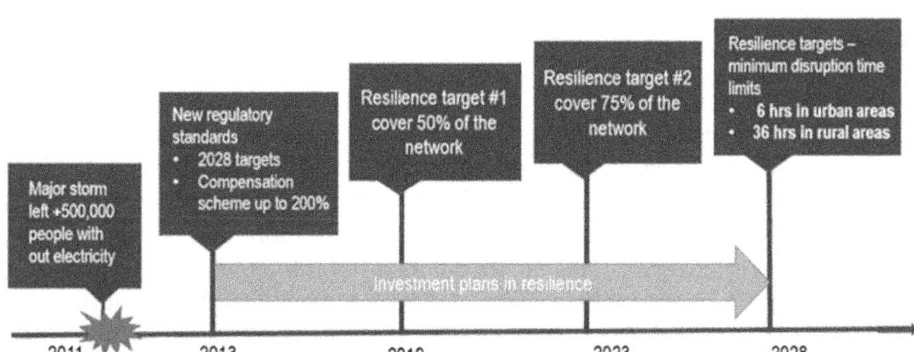

The system of sectoral pools coordinated by NESA was key to fostering trust among electricity stakeholders and build consensus on these resilience objectives

The governance approach to strengthening resilience of the energy network in Finland emphasizes a voluntary framework and cooperation between industry and sectoral government authorities. The Power and District Heating Pool has a dedicated sub-group on electricity transmission and distribution, which brings together all actors in the industry, authorities and the regulator on a voluntary basis to share information, foster preparedness and engage in policy design. Led by the industry – the TSO Fingrid being its chair – the pool is independent to designate its membership and its tasks are defined in a contract signed with NESA. There are strong incentives for operators to take part in the pooling system because of a wide range of benefits from information resources, sharing best practices and participation in trainings. NESA provides the necessary infrastructure for information-sharing and supports the activities of the pool.

Regular meetings and institutionalized dialogue within the Power and District Heating Pool allowed for the building of a shared vision of risks and resilience objectives between the public and private sector, and significantly contributed to the design of the revised legislation. Operators and government agree on the importance to secure power supply and ensure the continuity of services, however their views on the resilience levels that should be targeted and the ways to achieve them may differ. The pooling system provides a pathway to build consensus about resilience policies and objectives by engaging industry with sectoral authorities. This interaction proved valuable in the update of the regulatory standards in the Electricity Market Act in 2013. DSO's across Finland differ in size, capabilities and resources and bringing them together, as the pool has successfully achieved, helped stimulate open discussions on how to go about strengthening the networks' resilience. The large engagement in the pool demonstrates its success in developing trust between its participating stakeholders, which plays a key role in reaching common objectives. It helps also circumvent the potential risk of free-riding, as operators may feel peer-pressure from participating in regular discussions. According to the pool's participants, its discussions after the 2011 storm were fundamental to inform the design of the new resilience regulation, in a way that is consistent with operators' investments capacities, infrastructure assets' lifetime, and average profitability, as well as other policy priorities related to efficiency, innovation and climate change.

Resilience measures and their implementation

Risk assessments and information sharing across interdependent critical infrastructure

While the Finnish government conducts risk assessment and foresight analysis on future threats, there is no detailed interdependency mapping. The government utilises several tools to foster risk awareness of the whole-of-society, which provides useful information for electricity operators to anticipate major threats to the disruption of their networks. The Finnish National Risk Assessment is a cross-governmental tool that allows every 3 years to identify the most critical risks the country can face, their likelihood and potential impact (Box 4.2). Taking a forward-looking approach, NESA developed the Security of Supply 2030 scenarios, which presents five scenarios for the future and their implication for security of supply (NESA, 2018). Beyond building operators' awareness and anticipating potential cascading effects in these sets of scenarios, interdependency mapping and criticality assessments across critical infrastructure sectors is not yet conducted at the national level.

Operators have the responsibility to conduct criticality assessments of their network, but there is no single approach. In order to comply with regulations, operators are incentivised to conduct their own risk assessments to prioritise resilience measures and develop business continuity plans. The largest operators have adopted advanced risk modelling techniques in partnership with universities, allowing them to evaluate the impact of different risks on their network with a probabilistic method, for storms or floods for instance. International asset management standards such as ISO 55 000 are utilised to identify critical points in the network by others. While NESA has developed guidelines to support operators for their criticality assessment, there is no single approach to identify the most critical points, where failure could lead to the largest cascading consequences, including in other critical infrastructure sectors.

Information sharing within the Power and District Heating Pool provides opportunities for operators to learn about best approaches to risk assessment in a secured environment, but cross-sectoral exchange remains limited for interdependency analysis. Risk assessments can be strengthened by information-sharing platforms to share methods and technical expertise among operators. The pool's online platform encourages the ease and security of information sharing. Companies can access this online communication platform while NESA maintains the portal and ensures that information voluntarily provided will not be shared outside of safe circles. Guaranteeing security is an important factor to encourage sharing high quality information and maintaining trust in the pooling system. Otherwise, there is a risk that the information shared reveals business secrets or gets in the hands of malicious outside organizations. Pool members are thus required to sign confidentiality agreements to access the platform, and sensitivities can be flagged to NESA by businesses who want information to remain confidential. Cross-sectoral information sharing is encouraged, but the quality of information tends to decrease between pools. It will be important to facilitate more dialogue across pools to enhance understanding and analysis of interdependencies, especially given the criticality of the energy sector for all other critical infrastructure services, and the increasing cross dependencies with the IT sector.

Box 4.2. National risk assessment processes in Finland

The Finnish National Risk Assessment was conducted for the first time in 2015 by the Ministry of the Interior with a cross sectoral working group. The National Risk Assessment identifies the most important risks threatening people, the environment, property and critical systems and services that authorities need to prepare for. Based on an assessment of over 60 risk scenarios across all-hazards and threats, it selected 21 possible events defined either as wide-ranging events affecting society or as serious regional events. Information is provided on their potential impacts, likelihoods and measures taken to address these threats. It is worth noting that in the six wide-ranging events assessed, three scenario are related to electricity supply: serious disruption of energy supply, using the cyber domain in paralysing systems vital to society, and the risk of a solar storm. Similarly, among the serious regional events assessed, the large-scale winter storm is the one with the highest probability and largest impacts, and the scenario of several simultaneous major forest fires also considers electricity disruption as a potential impact.

The Finnish Security of Supply Scenarios 2030 were developed by NESA, as a foresight approach to future challenges. Its global five scenarios - Global interdependency, Armed power politics, Blocification and hybrid influence, Technological world order and Dominance of the East – propose possible development paths for the future informed by geopolitics, economic, demographic and technological trends. The document details out how the security of supply could be affected in these scenarios and proposes eight areas of action for both industries and the NESO to prepare for future challenges. These include adopting a system-thinking approach to security of supply, being attentive to the increased risks of cyber threats and hybrid influencing, and preparing for natural resource depletion, among others.

Source: (Ministry of Interior, 2016) (NESA, 2018)

In light of cyber risk specificities and the fast pace of change in this area, the pool established a dedicated sub-group for regular discussion and an early warning system when threats are detected. Cyber threats have received greater attention in recent years and demonstrated how they can potentially affect electricity transmission and distribution systems. While many electricity operators conduct dedicated risk analysis and strengthen their resilience measures internally, cooperation can help define the most relevant methods in this fast-changing environment. The pool established a dedicated forum on cyber security, with specific contact points in the companies to discuss assessment, prevention and situation awareness of cyber security incidents affecting electricity transmission and distribution. In partnership with the Cybersecurity Agency and the Energy Authority, to which mandatory reporting of cyber incidents is due by operators, NESA developed an early warning systems for cyber threats with secured communication channels to these contact points.

An important investment plan to increase the robustness of the electricity network is underway to comply with the new regulation

To reach the 2028 resilience targets, DSO's have the autonomy to decide on their preferred approach. They are required to submit an investment plan to the Energy Authority every two years demonstrating the progress made towards intermediary objectives. Estimates of the total investment for all DSO's are 9.5 billion euros, out of which 30% is for the extra level of resilience required by the revised regulation. The rest of investments are for normal renewal of ageing infrastructure and maintenance costs. For instance, the largest operator Caruna invested 1.2 billion euros since the 2011 storms in resilience and grid renewal and plans to invest 1 billion more by 2028. Another example comes from Helen Sähköverkko, the Helsinki metropolitan area operator, for which resilience has been a priority for a long time, and who says that the new regulations have not had a major effect on their investments. This can be explained by the fact that extreme storms have little effects on its largely urban network. The priority here is flood risks for which the long-term city flood strategic plan is in place where sub-stations are to be re-elevated when being renewed (City of Helsinki, 2013).

Measures to increase resilience of the energy network are diverse, but most DSOs choose the simplest but costly option of underground cabling especially in suburban areas. Operators can increase their network's resilience by strengthening robustness of the design such as underground cabling, expanding automation of the network and creating more redundancies with circular connections (Pantelli and Mancarella, 2017). Many DSO's are opting for underground cabling of medium to low voltage lines. Underground cabling is costly, but increases resilience of the network to weather related outages quickly. The target for 2028 is to ensure that 47% of medium voltage lines are placed underground. DSO's can set their own targets for their networks –companies operating in rural areas are estimated to transfer only 15-20% of the network underground and may opt for other measures. Other cost-efficient options include moving cable pathways from inside forests to open roads, or increasing the margin between trees and the cable lines by clearing out some parts of the forests (Figure 4.3). This is especially important in rural areas where overhead lines are located in areas difficult to reach and repair rapidly. Other more costly options involve building more substations to increase redundancies and reduce the scale of disruptions. For rural areas, where networks are mostly radial, this could be a measure to increase resilience. However, DSO's may not have sufficient resources to implement them. While the overall preference for underground cabling reflects market choices, the important investment it requires has led to increased costs for customers (see below). A scaled approach combining different set of measures could have been better accepted.

In addition, other resilience investments are made in the Finnish electricity transmission and distribution system, including by the transmission operator Fingrid for the main grid, as well as in cyber resilience. As per the Energy Market Act, Fingrid also submits its investment plan to the Energy Authority. According to its 2017-2027 investment plan, Fingrid will invest an average of 100 million euro per year in the next decade to maintain its resilience level and low transmission costs. This is a slight reduction compared to the previous investment period, during which interconnections with Sweden and Estonia increased financial needs significantly (Figure 4.4). This investment will be split almost equally between replacement of existing infrastructure and new substations and transmission lines, including for international connections with neighbouring Nordic countries. DSOs and Fingrid also implement resilience measures to increase cyber-security, such as strengthening firewalls, awareness measures for staff, and establishing cyber-security response teams.

Figure 4.3. Resilience measures in the electricity network

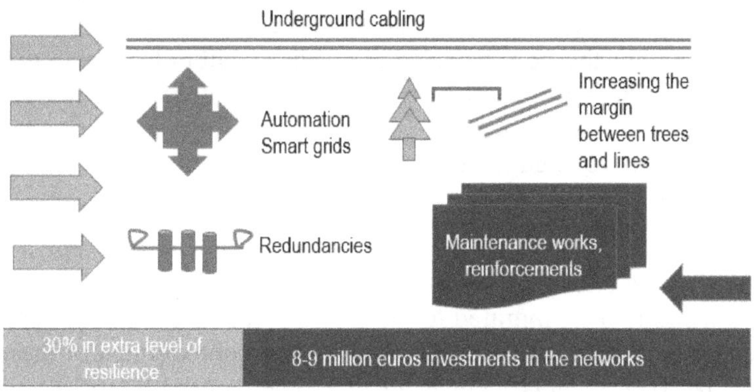

Underground cabling
Automation
Smart grids
Increasing the margin between trees and lines
Redundancies
Maintenance works, reinforcements
30% in extra level of resilience
8-9 million euros investments in the networks

Figure 4.4. Fingrid's investment levels in 2000–2027 in million euro

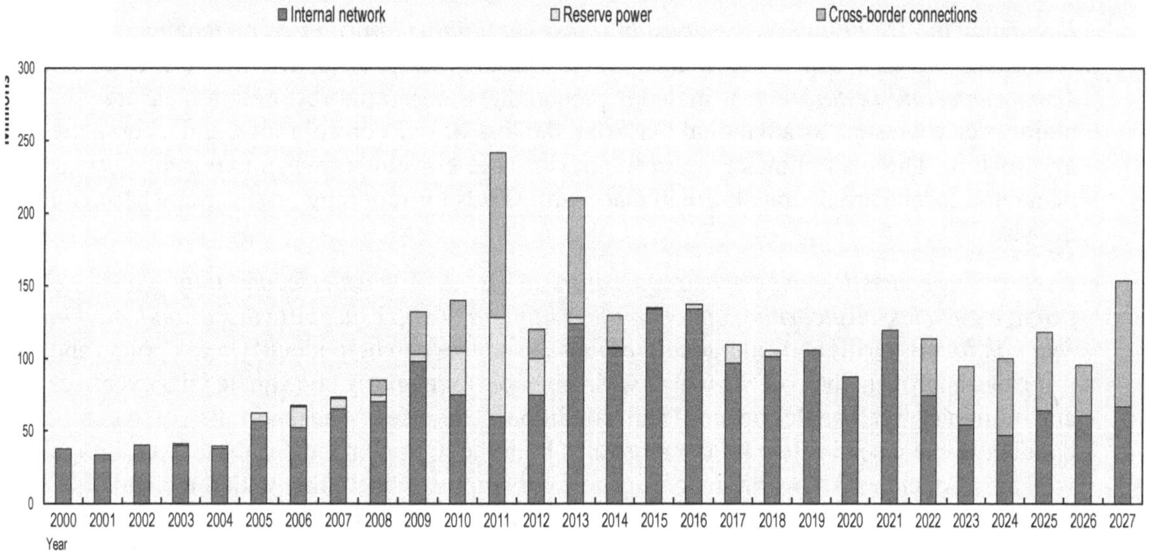

Source: (Fingrid, N.D.)

NESA's support to business continuity planning and the organisation of joint exercises, trainings and lessons learning is highly valued by electricity operators to strengthen their resilience.

NESA's expertise in emergency preparedness helps electricity operators to develop business continuity plans aimed at maintaining service and restoring rapidly operations in case of disruptions. The Electricity Market Act requires DSOs and the TSO to draw up business continuity plans under normal and emergency conditions, which must be tested and updated at least once every 3 years. Business continuity plans look at critical load points and how to prepare in case of incidents. They further develop lines of responsibilities, operational measures, and communication channels for emergency response. NESA has been supporting their development for many years through guidelines, trainings, advisory capacities, and assessment of the plans. Operators find the self-assessment tool for business continuity management that NESA has developed particularly useful. The self-assessment tool assesses these plans and makes comparison with the general trend within the pool so that operators can benchmark their results among their peers. Discussions within the pool has also allowed operators to realise that they are at times counting on similar resources to support their continuity (e.g. service providers), which could question the effectiveness of these plans in case of a large-scale outage. This has not yet led operators to engage in mutual aid agreements, as set up in some OECD countries (Asgary et al., 2017).

A new division of role between NESA and the regulator regarding approval of operators' continuity plans provides clarity on their respective role. Last year, the decision was made that these plans will now be submitted to the Energy Authority for their approval, while NESA and the pool will continue steering progress and improvement of these plans. This division of roles between voluntary engagement and support with NESA and the pool on one side, and oversight of mandatory requirements by the regulator on the other side appears as a good governance model to support resilience in the electricity transmission and distribution sector. Going forward, publicly disclosing some of the benchmark results could be another incentive for operators to further improve their preparedness.

Regarding the TSO Fingrid, its robust business continuity plan is based on the objective to restore its network within 24 hours after a blackout, as per the EU network code on 1emergency and restoration. It includes preparedness and rapid restoration measures for major accidents, such as a national blackout, the loss of one control room, and a complete loss of ICT. The plan allows Fingrid to cut off large consumers when major disruptions occur and special arrangements are in place with DSOs for rationing of electricity based on quotas.

Exercises organised by NESA help operators to test their business continuity plans and provide good lessons learning opportunities within the pool, especially those conducted in real conditions. Drills and emergency response exercises can help identify weak points and prioritise improvements. NESA works with the pools to regularly coordinate joint exercises and trainings, both table-top and real conditions exercises. The short list of recently conducted exercises in Box 4.3 demonstrates both the high demand for these exercises as well as the openness of operators to prepare for disruptions, including with the population. Complementary sharing of lessons learned from real incidents among operators fosters resilience improvements, and reflect the strong culture of transparency within the participants in the pool system.

Transboundary cooperation with Nordic countries and in Europe constitutes fundamental elements of Finland's approach to security of supply in the electricity sector.

NESA and Fingrid engage in bilateral and multilateral cooperation to support the resilience of the electricity system in Finland because of its important dependency on electricity imports in winter time and of the need to cooperate in case of a transboundary crisis. The Nordic Cooperation on emergency planning and crisis management for the power sector (NordBER) provides a framework for preparedness against power disruptions across Denmark, Finland, Iceland, Norway and Sweden (NordBER, 2015). NordBER facilitates regular meetings between the TSOs and the respective national authorities responsible for electricity transmission and distribution contingency and preparedness issues for information exchange, regional drills and exercises, and policy coordination. The NordBER framework has allowed setting-up a cross-border coordination mechanisms in the case of large-scale energy shortage affecting one of its members. Fingrid is part of the Nord Pool wholesale electricity market and engages in the TSO community with neighbouring countries on the balancing of power. The company also works with its neighbours on strengthening cross border interconnections. The Finnish and Swedish TSOs have decided to move forward with the implementation of the third alternating current connection with the aim of taking it into use by the end of 2025. The replacement of the Fenno-Skan 1 interconnector between Sweden and Finland is under consideration for an investment in the late 2020s.

Box 4.3. Security of supply exercises recently conducted by NESA on electricity transmission and distribution disruption

Table-top exercises included for instance a black out affecting one town with the objective to balance production and consumption. Another exercise conducted in 2017 was to test how authorities would react in case of a disruption of electricity for two weeks, with a focus on communication methods and channels. In 2019, similar exercises will be implemented regionally. A real condition exercise in Lapland was carried out in 2014 with an arranged black out in one city for one hour resulting in a conclusion that it could take a day to restore power supply nationally. In Helsinki, an exercise of a half-hour to some hours black out in a large part of the city will be conducted soon.

Source: Interviews conducted by OECD, 2018

Governance effectiveness for resilience and challenges for the future

The revised governance model for power supply resilience in Finland shows great results in its first years of implementation

Finland's governance model for the resilience of its electricity transmission and distribution system combines the power of a strong regulatory framework and a well-established cooperative model between the public and private sector to reach ambitious resilience targets. The 2013 Electricity Market Act, the pooling system, and the support of NESA provide together a comprehensive set of incentives for electricity operators to invest in resilience. The clear definition of roles between the regulator and NESA demonstrates the coherence of this stick and carrot approach to foster resilience: on one side, the Energy Authority oversees compliance with resilience regulations, and on the other side NESA facilitates the voluntary engagement of operators in resilience actions through a series of information-sharing, guidance, and peer-review tools. This appears as a good policy response to the large-scale disruptions caused by the Tapani storm in 2011, as well as to adjust to a dynamic risk landscape marked by increased interdependencies, climate change and rising concerns over cyber and hybrid threats.

The on-going implementation of this resilience policy shows a large engagement of the different operators who appear to adhere to both its objectives and approach. The pool system functions well and allows secured information-sharing as well as the co-construction of policies and implementation tools. NESA's guidance and tools are utilised by operators, who largely participate in its activities. Operators are investing in the robustness of their network as per the regulation, which is well tailored to foster these investments: some operators calculated that the level of compensations they might have to pay to customers could reach one fourth of their turnover in case of a storm similar to

Tapani. In addition, the new policy created momentum for resilience investments targeted at other risks such as cyber.

As this approach starts having cost implications for customers, balancing public expectations on resilience versus price increase would require a close monitoring of the cost-effectiveness of resilience investments.

Resilience investments start having cost implications for customers, which would need to be closely monitored to ensure continuous public acceptance of this ambitious policy for the security of the country. Regarding compensation, the new scheme was first activated during the January 2018 winter storm, which left 40 000 people without electricity in northern Finland - some up to a week. As a result, 10 000 customers received compensation up to a total of 5 million euros. On the other hand, investments made in robustness led DSOs to improve in parallel the quality of their services, which per the regulation allowed them to raise distribution prices. In its 2017 yearly report, the Energy Authority indicated that household consumers saw a distribution price increase of 5.4% on average compared to the previous year (Energy Authority, 2017). In some instances, the increase reached 30%. Strong public and political reaction led to the adjusting of the Electricity Market Act to cap yearly price increase at 15%, which can create cash-flow problems for some operators. Transmission costs, while they remain low per European standards, have gone up two-fold over the last 10 years.

This demonstrates the importance of carefully considering public expectations and their change overtime when designing resilience policy instruments, as well as to conduct a close dialogue with operators on the most affordable ways to increase resilience. There should be an optimal balance between costs, investments and reliability of services, in order to ensure both that public expectations on the reliability of power are met and that cost increases remain acceptable. In the aftermath of the 2010 and 2011 storms, society expressed a high demand for improved reliability levels. Policy-makers responded with the ambitious objectives set in the revised Electricity Market Act, which operators acted upon by investing in resilience. As the memory of this disaster slowly fades away, so does the willingness to pay. While it is essential to maintain a stable regulatory environment in this sector where long-term investments are needed, there could be a way to discuss with operators on the cost-effectiveness of the resilience measures they take. Complementary solutions to underground cabling might be cheaper.

Differences between transmission operators' resources and capacities has implications on the way they implement resilience measures across the country and its overall resilience

The large diversity among the 77 DSOs operating in Finland means that they have varying capabilities and resources to meet the 2028 resilience targets. The largest operators often cover densely populated urban areas. They have mobilised significant resources to invest in resilience and are on a good track to meet targets. On the other side, the smallest operators in rural and isolated parts of the country face financial constraints and technical difficulties to do so. Large operators, those with private shareholding in particular, are maximising their profitability within the new regulatory framework. This explains why underground cabling in the densest part of the country has been the most prevalent option so far and fits well with the priority established on the most critical points of the network. Nevertheless, there are concerns over the growing disparities in terms of resilience of distribution networks across the Finnish territory. In remote areas, electricity cuts can generate significant impact for the populations, with long restoration times, which may call into question the overall benefits of the new regulation. On the other hand, smaller DSOs fully benefit from the exchange of good practices from their peers within the pool system, to improve their awareness and structure their business continuity plans, including those for cyber risks.

Going forward, preparations for future updates of the governance model could reflect upon ways to support the resilience of small DSOs. Other cost-efficient options are available besides underground cabling, such as setting up more redundancies, removing trees from the lines or other innovative solutions. In this case, co-financing options could be explored to complement market-based solutions, as a way to ensure that all DSO's have the opportunity to reach resilience targets.

Future-proofing power supply in Finland would require more joint action with interdependent sectors, as well as to further connect policy agendas on innovation, climate and resilience.

NESA's drive towards a system-approach to the governance of critical infrastructure resilience does not yet materialise in cross-sectoral cooperation, which is particularly important between the electricity and ICT sectors. As flagged in the NESA Security of Supply Scenario 2030, the electricity sector is currently going through transformative changes, and these will affect security of supply (NESA, 2018). Mutual interdependencies between electricity transmission and distribution and the ICT sector are rising fast, with the deployment of automated control systems and smart grids by DSOs and TSO. However, continuity requirements differ between the two sectors, investment time-lines and returns do not align, and information exchange between the respective pools is not optimal. Interdependency mapping could be improved to jointly strengthen the resilience of these sectors to common risks, from telecommunication or electricity outages to cyber-attacks. In light of the disruptions experienced after the Tapani storm in 2011, there is room to leverage the pooling system to foster cross-sectoral information sharing, facilitate in-depth analysis of resilience, interdependencies, and critical failure points between sectors, as well as prepare a multi-sectoral resilience action plan.

Other transformative changes in the energy sector driven by innovation and climate change provide opportunities for improving resilience but could also challenge security of supply and operators business models. Finland's climate strategy proposes a strong increased of renewable energy to replace coal generation, and the deployment of smart systems is central to its innovation strategy. On one side, these evolutions could result in increased flexibility and back-up capacities to balance supply and demand, and facilitate network's operations. On the other side, more intermittent production and off-grid local generation and distribution are raising concerns on security of supply. There is a risk that returns on the on-going investments in the resilience of electricity network might be lower than expected, if these new capacities are not utilised as planned. There is a need for all stakeholders in the pool as well as at the policy level to carefully reflect on how DSOs and TSO resilience business models could be affected by these evolutions.

Box 4.4. Recommendation for Finland

For strengthening the resilience of its critical infrastructure in the electricity transmission and distribution sector, Finland could consider the following set of recommendations:

1. Maintain a continuous dialogue with operators on the cost-effectiveness of the resilience measures they take to foster diversification of solutions.
2. Strengthen awareness of the population on risks to network disruptions and communicate progress made on resilience to facilitate societal acceptance of cost increases.
3. Explore options to further support smaller operators in their efforts to reach resilience targets.
4. Leverage the cooperative model of the pooling system to strengthen interdependency analysis and joint action between the electricity and the ICT sectors.

Facilitate the development of mutual aid agreements between operators on a voluntary basis.

References

Asgary, A. et al. (2017), "Developing disaster mutual aid decision criteria for electricity industry", *Disaster Prevention and Management: An International Journal*, Vol. 26/2, pp. 230-240, https://www.emeraldinsight.com/doi/pdfplus/10.1108/DPM-05-2016-0107.

City of Helsinki (2013), *The City of Helsinki Instructions on Prevention and Control of Floods: Protection of residents and property in flood hazards areas in Helsinki*, https://www.hel.fi/static/helsinki/julkaisut/Tulvaohje_eng_17062013.pdf.

Energy Authority (2017), *National Report 2017 to the Agency for the Cooperation of Energy*, Energy Authority, Finland, https://www.energiavirasto.fi/documents/10191/0/National_Report_2017_Finland_1469-401-2017.pdf/6b783563-e997-4c4c-ace9-826d68447c9b.

Fingrid (2018), *Risk of electricity shortage in Finland on Thursday, 19 July*, https://www.fingrid.fi/en/pages/news/news/2018/risk-of-electricity-shortage-in-finland-on-thursday-19-july/.

Fingrid (N.D.), *Main grid development plan 2017-2027*, https://www.fingrid.fi/globalassets/dokumentit/fi/kantaverkko/kantaverkon-kehittaminen/main-grid-development-plan-2017-2027.pdf.

Forssen, K. (2016), *Resilience of Finnish electricity distribution networks against*, https://aaltodoc.aalto.fi/bitstream/handle/123456789/19983/master_Forss%E9n_Kim_2016.pdf?sequence=1.

Kufeoglu, S. and M. Lehtonen (2014), *Cyclone Dagmar of 2011 and its impacts in Finland*, http://dx.doi.org/10.1109/ISGTEurope.2014.7028868.

Ministry of Economic Affairs and Employment (2013), *The Electricity Market Act 588/2013 [Sähkömarkkinalaki]*, https://www.finlex.fi/fi/laki/alkup/2013/20130588 (accessed on 28 November 2018).

Ministry of Employment and the Economy (2013), *Government Decision on the Security of Supply Goals*, https://s3-eu-west-1.amazonaws.com/huoltovarmuuskeskus/app/uploads/2016/08/31144502/2013-12-05_Government_decision_on_the_security_of_supply_goals.pdf?AWSAccessKeyId=AKIAITCZYCPQYFESGSAQ&Expires=1543875271&Signature=M5SLweaiUDfXX0gsE77JXW84EPc%3D.

Ministry of Interior (2016), *National Risk Assessment 2015*, http://dx.doi.org/978-952-324-060-5.

Ministry of the Envrionment (2017), *Government Report on Medium-term Climate Change Policy Plan for 2030: Towards Climate-Smart Day-to-Day Living*, http://julkaisut.valtioneuvosto.fi/handle/10024/80703.

NESA (2018), *Security of Supply: Scenarios 2030*, https://s3-eu-west-1.amazonaws.com/huoltovarmuuskeskus/app/uploads/2018/09/06091431/Eng-Scenarios-2030.pdf?AWSAccessKeyId=AKIAITCZYCPQYFESGSAQ&Expires=1543553617&Signature=GkvOd%2BzJLB1BqTw2oPqgCKqzEQE%3D.

NordBER (2015), *Energy shortage Coordinated handling of a potential disturbance in the Nordic power system*, https://www.energimyndigheten.se/globalassets/trygg-energiforsorjning/el/energy-shortage---coordinated-handling-of-a-potential-disturbance-in-the-nordic-power-system.pdf.

OECD (2014), *Recommendation of the Council on the Governance of Critical Risks*, OECD Publishing, http://www.oecd.org/gov/risk/Critical-Risks-Recommendation.pdf.

Bugliarello, G. and C. Arenberg (eds.) (2007), *Critical Infrastructure, Interdependencies, and Resilience*, National Academy of Engineering, https://www.nae.edu/File.aspx?id=7405&v=70df971.

Pantelli, M. and P. Mancarella (2017), "Modelling and Evaluating the Resilience of Critical Electrical Power Infrastructure to Extreme Weather Events", *IEE Systems Journal*, Vol. 11/3, pp. 1733-1742, https://www.researchgate.net/profile/Mathaios_Panteli/publication/272364268_Modeling_and_Evaluating_the_Resilience_of_Critical_Electrical_Power_Infrastructure_to_Extreme_Weather_Events/links/57356e6408ae9ace8409609a/Modeling-and-Evaluating-the-Resilience-.

The Security Committee (2017), *Security Strategy for Society*, https://turvallisuuskomitea.fi/wp-content/uploads/2018/04/YTS_2017_english.pdf.

Law, T. (ed.) (2018), *Electricity regulation in Finland*, https://uk.practicallaw.thomsonreuters.com/7-629-2923?transitionType=Default&contextData=(sc.Default)&firstPage=true&comp=pluk&bhcp=1.

North, R. (2019), [illegible]

5. Policy Toolkit on Governance of Critical Infrastructure Resilience

This chapter presents the OECD Policy Toolkit on Governance of Critical Infrastructure Resilience that can inspire governments' policy reforms towards improved continuity of these essential services. Developed in the context of the OECD High-Level Risk Forum, this Toolkit provides a comprehensive policy framework to strengthen critical infrastructure resilience and overcome related governance challenges. The Toolkit emphasizes the importance of adopting a system approach for critical infrastructure resilience, based on partnerships between governments and critical infrastructure operators.

Context for the development of the OECD Policy Toolkit

This chapter presents the OECD Policy Toolkit on Governance of Critical Infrastructure Resilience, developed through the OECD High-Level Risk Forum (HLRF). The HLRF brings together government officials to identify and share good practices in deepening the understanding of emerging and complex risks, and to share good practices in their governance and management. It invites experts from the private sector, civil society, think tanks and academia to identify gaps in risk governance and to explore solutions to current and future challenges. The HLRF takes an inclusive approach to policy analysis, which reflects its suggested best practice as embodied in the OECD Recommendation on the Governance of Critical Risks, adopted by the OECD Council in 2014 (OECD, 2014[1]).

Due to the high economic costs and social harms that disruptions to critical infrastructure produce, the OECD Recommendation underlines the importance for governments to reinforce resilience and security in critical infrastructure networks. In 2016, the OECD conducted a survey to take stock of implementation of the OECD Recommendation by Adherents. The survey results revealed that a major hurdle to implementation of the Recommendation is sharing responsibility between governments and businesses to protect critical infrastructure assets and ensure quick restoration of service (OECD, 2018[2]).

To address this challenge, the High-Level Risk Forum called for the OECD to conduct research and develop a good practice report on how governments and businesses can structure effective partnerships in building more secure and resilient critical infrastructure. Further to this call, the OECD ran a cross-country survey on critical infrastructure resilience, organized thematic workshops, conducted regional research projects and pilot country case-studies, and contributed to relevant OECD multidisciplinary activities. These activities helped deepen the evidence base on critical infrastructure resilience presented in this report and extend the OECD network of policymakers with responsibility for critical infrastructure, as well as regulators, operators from the public and private sectors and researchers working on this topic.

The process began with a stocktaking report, which was discussed at the High-Level Risk Forum in 2017 and constitutes the basis of this report. The Forum agreed for OECD to organise a dedicated workshop on "System-thinking for Critical Infrastructure Resilience and Security" in partnership with the European Commission's Joint Research Centre (OECD and EU JRC, 2018[41]). The workshop took place on 23-24 September 2018 with a focus on tools, methodologies and data requirements to assess system's resilience and on the policy instruments that governments can mobilise for critical infrastructure resilience. Participants suggested that the OECD High-Level Risk Forum develop a "Policy Toolkit on Governance of Critical Infrastructure Resilience" based on the workshop's discussions and OECD analysis.

Policy challenges for critical infrastructure resilience

Recent shock events caused by natural hazards, industrial accidents, cyber-threats, or other security risks, illustrate how disruptions to key systems and essential services, such as water, energy, transport or information and telecommunication systems can result in substantial economic damage, in addition to loss of lives in some cases. The interconnectedness of supply chains, technological and financial systems, which form the foundation of the global economy, increases critical infrastructure exposure and vulnerability to such unanticipated events, yielding negative impacts across sectors and borders, which at times can resonate globally. This hyper-connectivity between infrastructure assets, sectors and countries calls for comprehensive public policies to strengthen critical infrastructure resilience and limit the risk of disruptions of the essential services they provide.

Beginning in the 2000s, several governments established public policies to promote protection of critical infrastructure and actions to implement them. Generally, these include an effort to define critical infrastructure sectors, the development of an inventory of critical infrastructure assets and adopting regulations, national programmes or incentive mechanisms to strengthen the resilience of these assets. However, critical infrastructure protection policies have not always proven to be sufficiently effective to address challenges of the 21st century risk landscape.

The diversity and complexity of shock events, the increased interdependences and interconnectedness, climate change, the fast pace of innovation that fundamentally transforms critical infrastructure sectors, as well as ageing infrastructure, are among the challenges with which critical infrastructure resilience policies have to contend. Many researchers on this topic conclude that a shift in focus from protection to resilience would help policymakers to better account for uncertainty by integrating concepts such as adaptability, flexibility and robustness into the design of critical infrastructure and their regulatory frameworks.

Following the adoption of the OECD Recommendation on the Governance of Critical Risks, several international fora gave recognition to the importance of infrastructure resilience. The G7 Ise-Shima Principles for Promoting Quality Infrastructure Investments emphasizes resilience against natural hazards , terrorism and cyber-attack risks to ensure reliable operation and economic efficiency in view of life-cycle cost (G7, 2016[38]). Similarly, the UN Sendai Framework for Disaster Risk Reduction calls countries to "substantially reduce disaster damage to critical infrastructure and disruption of basic services" (United Nations Office for Disaster Risk Reduction, 2015[39]). The OECD Framework on the Governance of Infrastructure also highlights infrastructure resilience as one if its 10 key governance challenges (OECD, 2017[11]).

Today there is strong demand for practical policy guidance to enhance resilience throughout the life-cycle of critical infrastructure. Governments and infrastructure stakeholders are facing key governance challenges when it comes to investing in resilience and designing relevant policies. Evidence-based guidance and the sharing of good practices across countries can provide useful insights in response to challenging questions such as:

- What is the proper role for governments in boosting critical infrastructure resilience?
- How can governments effectively engage critical infrastructure operators – public and private – in strengthening their resilience efforts?
- What are the most appropriate mechanisms to share sensitive information about risks, vulnerabilities, and resilience measures between government and operators?
- How to share costs and benefits of investing in resilience between governments, operators and end-users?

The recent increase of infrastructure investments globally, digitalisation and a changing risk landscape provide opportunities to rethink critical infrastructure policies across OECD countries and beyond, and to integrate resilience in upfront planning and designs.

Box 5.1. System approach for critical infrastructure policies

To shift from a protection centric strategy to one that emphasizes resilience, critical infrastructure policies need to feature the following qualities from a system-thinking perspective:

- **All-hazards and threats**: Single-hazard policies are not sufficient to build infrastructure resilience. An all-hazards and threats forward-looking approach to critical infrastructure resilience and security enables policy makers and operators to better prepare for the unexpected.
- **System-level**: Infrastructure assets are usually only the components of a wider complex system, which should be considered in its entirety in a comprehensive resilience strategy. A system approach allows for prioritising the most critical components, and addresses weak points that create critical vulnerabilities for the entire system.
- **Multi-sectoral coordination**: Addressing interdependencies in policies requires policy makers and operators to go beyond a silo-based approach and to target the critical infrastructure sectors together. While operators tend to be well aware of their own dependencies upon critical sectors, they may not be as conscious of the dependencies others have upon their own services.
- **Public-private cooperation**: Although governments continue to own, invest in, and operate critical infrastructure in some sectors, a large share of critical infrastructure is either privately owned or operated. The resilience of these systems depends upon governments partnering with infrastructure operators from the public and private sectors in resilience efforts through the establishment of relevant governance arrangements.
- **Life-cycle approach**: Different resilience measures may apply at different phases of the infrastructure life-cycle: robustness and redundancies requires investments in the design phase, while business continuity planning and maintenance pertains to the operations, and adaptability can be based on infrastructure retrofitting. Thus, it is important to set-up a comprehensive policy that enables resilience throughout infrastructure life-cycle.
- **Entire risk management cycle**: A comprehensive resilience policy should incorporate measures throughout the entire risk management cycle, from risk assessment, to risk prevention, emergency preparedness, response, recovery and reconstruction.
- **Risk-based and layered approach**: Given the considerable degree of uncertainty about future risks, the manifold dimensions of infrastructure systems vulnerability, and all the interrelationships between these systems, the prioritisation of resilience measures is essential. A risk-based and layered approach helps account for complex interdependencies, for all-hazards and across the infrastructure life-cycle.
- **Transboundary dimension**: Risks arising from interdependencies and interconnectedness cannot be fully mitigated without incorporating their international dimension. Fostering international cooperation is key to infrastructure resilience.

Objectives of the Policy Toolkit

The aim of the Policy Toolkit on Governance of Critical Infrastructure Resilience is to help governments design their national critical infrastructure resilience policies and implement them through effective partnerships with operators.

It proposes practical guidance, supported by country good practices and indicative benchmark indicators, which governments can use to:

- Identify critical infrastructure, map out (inter-)dependencies and prioritise the critical services and functions, systems, and assets, where investments in resilience and security are the most required.
- Forge effective partnerships with critical infrastructure operators to build mutual trust, share information on risks and vulnerabilities and agree on a common vision and policy objectives.
- Share responsibilities to protect critical infrastructure assets and ensure quick restoration of service.

The Policy Toolkit proposes that governments adopt a system approach to critical infrastructure resilience, i.e. their policies should address all-hazards and threats, ensure multi-sectoral coordination and public-private cooperation, integrate planning for the whole infrastructure life-cycle, target measures across the risk management cycle and foster transboundary cooperation (Box 5.1).

Going forward, the OECD will work with the High-Level Risk Forum to support countries' implementation of this Policy Toolkit and benchmark their progress in increasing the resilience of critical infrastructure.

Policy toolkit on governance of critical infrastructure resilience

Definitions

It proposes to use the following definitions:

- **Critical infrastructure**: Critical infrastructure are systems, assets, facilities and networks that provide essential services for the functioning of the economy and the safety and well-being of the population. While definitions of critical infrastructure differ across countries, this definition is not prescriptive and aims to encompass the largest set of definitions identified in the OECD Survey on Critical Infrastructure Resilience.
- **Resilience**: the capacity of systems to absorb a disturbance, recover from disruptions and adapt to changing conditions while retaining essentially the same function as prior to the disruptive shock (adapted from OECD, 2014[20]). This definition includes the ability to withstand shocks with as little loss of functionality as possible under the specific circumstances, limiting the duration of potential service interruption by minimising the recovery time, as well as adapting to new conditions and improving systems' functionality.

Seven steps for critical infrastructure resilience policies

To strengthen critical infrastructure resilience, a comprehensive policy framework should address the following seven interrelated governance challenges:

1. Setting up a multi-sector governance structure for critical infrastructure resilience
2. Understanding complex interdependencies and vulnerabilities across infrastructure systems to prioritise resilience efforts
3. Establishing trust between government and operators by securing risk-related information-sharing
4. Building partnerships to agree on a common vision and achievable resilience objectives
5. Defining the policy mix to prioritise cost-effective resilience measures across the life-cycle
6. Ensuring accountability and monitoring implementation of critical infrastructure resilience policies
7. Addressing the transboundary dimension of infrastructure systems

1. Setting up a multi-sector governance structure for critical infrastructure resilience

Governments should adopt a whole-of-government approach to critical infrastructure resilience. Ideally, such governance would involve the sectoral ministries and agencies overseeing infrastructure delivery and regulation in the multiple critical sectors, as well as those in charge of resilience to all-hazards and threats. Coordination at the Center-of-Government would allow to manage the interests of all stakeholders and make the relevant trade-offs for effective resilience policies.

Why is this important?

Governments have a key role to play in critical infrastructure resilience. They have a responsibility to provide security and safety to citizens, and are often infrastructure regulators. Governments, at central or sub-national level, can also be owners and operators of critical infrastructure, either directly or through publicly owned companies. Furthermore, investments in major infrastructure are often dependent upon major public funds. Finally, governments are also an important user or client of critical infrastructure, with expectations on their reliability for the continuity of government activities.

This presents governments with multiple and complex roles, across critical infrastructure sectors and for multiple hazards and threats. Risk managers and officials in charge of the governance of critical risks have to coordinate across several functions in government and ensure that, on behalf of the general interest, policy objectives can be achieved from a resilience perspective while balancing the relevant trade-offs.

Key policy questions:

- *Is there a national strategy or policy document for critical infrastructure resilience?*
- *Is there a definition for critical infrastructure?*
- *Is a pre-defined list of critical infrastructure sectors in place?*
- *Is there a whole-of-government approach to the development of critical infrastructure resilience?*
- *Are all relevant hazards and threats considered in the critical infrastructure resilience policy?*

- *Is there a dedicated coordination entity responsible for designing, monitoring and adjusting the national critical infrastructure resilience policy?*

Benchmark indicators

- *National policy on critical infrastructure resilience*
- *Inter-departmental / ministerial committee / platform to design CI resilience policies*
- *Coordination entity at the Center of Government*

Examples of good practices

- *In the United States, the Presidential Policy Directive on Critical Infrastructure Security and Resilience tasks the Department of Homeland Security to coordinate CI policies at Federal level with sector agencies across 16 CI sectors.*
- *In France, the General Secretariat for Defense and National Security under the Prime Minister coordinates the CI resilience policy across 8 line Ministries for 12 infrastructure sectors and with a multi-hazard approach.*

2. Understanding complex (inter-)dependencies and vulnerabilities across critical infrastructure systems to prioritise resilience efforts

Governments should adopt methodologies and metrics to identify the critical functions, systems and assets that should be prioritised for investments in building resilience. This requires a good understanding of how disruptions can affect infrastructure assets and where dependencies and interdependencies are found that could amplify their impacts. Once priority nodes and hubs are identified across interdependent systems, there is a need to assess their resilience with relevant indicators and to compare actual and expected results to see where the gaps are.

Why is this important?

Defining methodologies for risk assessment that critical infrastructure stakeholders from government and operators can use in practice and clarifying the related data requirements are fundamental steps to prioritise investments in resilience. Understanding risks and vulnerabilities of critical infrastructures is a complex task, given the underlying interdependencies and requires a systemic view. A diverse set of tools exists to identify critical assets, understand their vulnerabilities to shock events and model the potential cascading impacts through interconnected networks. Recent research has focused on system complexity, risk modelling, and interdependency mapping, which provides rich analytical materials.

Nevertheless, governments and critical infrastructure operators are grappling with the need to choose the right tools for the identification of the most critical hubs and nodes of infrastructure systems and the assessment of their level of resilience. In practice, such analysis follows a three-tier approach, for which methodologies and tools need to be standardised. First, mapping the interdependencies (physical, digital, geographic, logical) between critical infrastructure assets and systems is key to estimating the full impact of service loss in case of disruption. Second, conducting a criticality assessment allows to classify systems, networks, and asset that are truly critical, based on the impact of their disruption on a range of pre-established criteria. Third, resilience analysis and stress-tests help identify weak points where potential failures are more likely to happen. Developing relevant indicators for infrastructure assets and systems enables the best comparison of their level of resilience.

Key policy questions:

- *Is there a mapping of dependencies and interdependencies across the different critical infrastructure sectors?*
- *Are there defined criteria to assess the criticality of infrastructures?*
- *Are there multi-hazards stress tests conducted to identify weak points among critical infrastructure?*

Benchmark indicators

- *Identification of critical assets*
- *Existence of resilience indicators*

Examples of good practices

- *In the Netherlands, the National Coordinator for Security and Counterterrorism (NCTV) developed a 3-step methodology to first identify critical infrastructure and categorise them according to their criticality (A or B), second assess their vulnerabilities to multiple risks and third set priorities for resilience investments.*
- *Public Safety Canada (PSC) has undertaken high-level inter-dependency analyses of individual CI sectors with examination of cascading impacts. PSC is evaluating critical infrastructure inter-dependency modelling tools developed by the research community.*

3. Establishing trust between governments and operators and securing information-sharing on risks and vulnerabilities

Governments should establish information-sharing platforms with operators of critical infrastructure so that all relevant infrastructure stakeholders obtain a comprehensive and shared understanding of risks and vulnerabilities to conduct resilience analysis. It is crucial to ensure that the design of these platforms assures security and confidentiality of information shared with clear rules of access to allow a trusted sharing of sensitive information.

Why is this important?

Information exchange is fundamental for governments to gain a comprehensive understanding of critical infrastructure vulnerabilities. It also helps operators to understand their own vulnerabilities, their dependencies on other infrastructures, and how disruptions to their services could affect other infrastructures or even themselves.

The challenge to fostering information-sharing is to build trust between parties, such that the security and proprietary of information shared voluntarily will not be publicly disclosed. Operators are not inclined to share sensitive information about their vulnerabilities, their critical dependencies and any disruptive incidents outside of safe circles, as disclosure of certain information may lead to liability, be important for competitiveness in the market or do damage to a firm's reputation. On the government side, information-sharing may involve classified information when it relates to national security. Risks of cyber threats are another concern, as they can also increase reluctance to share information on joint platforms, if guarantees on their security are not properly assured.

In some cases, disclosure of risk information can strengthen operators' accountability and reinforce resilience measures, for climate-related risks for instance. In a world characterized by interconnected systems, the resilience of interdependent infrastructures is as strong as its weakest link. Therefore, information sharing significantly contributes to bringing infrastructure operators up to a similar understanding of what is required to reach an acceptable level of security and resilience.

Key questions:

- *Are there mandatory or voluntary legislation, regulations, and policies for information sharing about risks and vulnerabilities?*
- *Are there information-sharing platforms for governments and critical infrastructure operators?*
- *Are there incentives for infrastructure operators to share qualitative information about their dependencies and vulnerabilities with the policy community?*
- *Are there safeguards in place to secure the confidentiality of shared information?*

Benchmark indicators

- *Presence of a secured information sharing mechanism*
- *Frequency, quantity and quality of shared information from infrastructure operators*
- *Utilisation/satisfaction of the information sharing platform*

Examples of good practices

- The United Kingdom Data and Analytics Facility for National Infrastructure (DAFNI) provides *a platform of data, models and technical tools for complex infrastructure analysis to analyse system performance and make wise investments.*
- *Australia Trusted Information Sharing Network (TISN) for Critical Infrastructure provides national level forums for critical infrastructure operators to share vital information on risks and mitigation* strategies with in a secure, non-competitive environment, and to develop collective solutions to shared problems.

4. Building partnerships to agree on a common vision and achievable resilience objectives

Governments should partner with critical infrastructure operators from the public and the private sectors to agree on a common resilience vision for critical infrastructure nationwide and on shared and achievable resilience objectives. Developing an understanding of public expectations to potential loss of infrastructure service can be a useful way to initiate dialogue.

Why is this important?

Beyond information-sharing on risks and vulnerabilities, critical infrastructure resilience depends upon governments partnering with infrastructure operators from the public and private sectors in resilience efforts. While operators and governments agree on the need to protect critical assets and maintain their services, views can differ on the level of resilience required, the means to achieve it, and on the regulatory requirements that should apply. These measures have financial implications, and raise questions about who will take on additional costs to invest in resilience.

Establishing partnerships between governments and operators (public and private) to encourage dialogue on these issues is a useful approach to develop a common vision towards resilience in critical infrastructure and define shared objectives. Policy issues to be addressed include deciding on the acceptable duration of 'down time', maintaining a level-playing field between operators, and circumventing situations of free-riding in competitive sectors. Ensuring stakeholders' engagement, including with the public, in regular meetings, institutionalized dialogues, and joint exercises can foster consensus.

Key policy questions:

- *Are there institutionalised dialogues in place to engage critical infrastructure operators in resilience policy design?*
- *Are there processes in place to understand public expectations for critical infrastructure resilience?*
- *Is there a common vision of critical infrastructure resilience defined through multi-sector dialogue?*
- *Are there resilience objectives established to support the vision's implementation?*

Benchmark indicators

- Existence *of critical infrastructure stakeholders consultation fora*
- *Frequency of consultation fora and level of operator's participation*
- *Quality of the participatory* process

Examples of good practices

- In Switzerland, the national CIP strategy coordinated by the Federal Office for Civil Protection is based on partnerships and various platforms with CI operators, *federal and subnational authorities. Beyond risk analysis and information sharing, the CI Guideline is developed jointly and allows setting resilience objectives for CI operators.*
- *In Germany, the UP KRITIS is a National initiative between the state and carriers of Critical* Infrastructures for the protection of critical information infrastructures. The UP KRITIS consists of more than 450 associates.

5. Defining the policy mix to prioritise cost-effective resilience measures across the life-cycle

Governments should define a mix of policy tools to incentivize operators' investments in resilience and achieve shared resilience objectives. Such measures should address the entire infrastructure life-cycle from planning to operations, maintenance and renewal or retrofitting. Government prioritisation of resilience measures should be informed by cost-benefit analysis taking into account repercussions on the cost of service.

Why is this important?

Governments can choose from a variety of policy tools and mechanisms to advance implementation of resilience objectives, from voluntary frameworks and incentive mechanisms, to regulatory or legal tools. Operators have a keen interest in maintaining the continuity of their services and their reputation by investing in resilience. However, investments in resilience often imply costs up front, even if these should be compensated in terms of greater reliability of service and resilience to shocks. The question is how to find the right balance. Additional requirements imposed by governments to strengthen resilience may result in additional costs ultimately borne by customers, citizens and businesses. It is important to tailor public policy instruments to provide effective incentives for operators to invest in resilience, while managing the financial repercussions.

The regulatory approach has strengths in that it provides clear and measurable obligations, for instance setting reliability requirements, or requiring business continuity plans, insurance mechanisms, and minimum security standards. However, when to prescriptive, it can also prove costly, not be up to speed with rapid technological developments and can create compliance challenges. Imposing a compensation scheme for customers whose service is disrupted, or other types of penalties can be efficient to incentivise resilience investments, notably in public-private-partnerships. Such approach also provides operators with the choice of the ways to increase their resilience. Voluntary frameworks such as the development of resilience guidelines, awareness raising activities or the sharing of good practices, is often a preferred option to favour stakeholder engagement, but has important uncertainties. Finding a balance between public financial support and private investments for such resilience measures, can use cost-benefit analysis methods to prioritise the most effective ways to share the costs of an overall collective effort towards achieving shared resilience objectives.

Key policy questions:

- *Are there resilience measures defined to increase the level of protection, robustness, redundancy or adaptability across critical infrastructure life cycle?*
- *Are there minimum security standards in place to ensure operators invest in resilience?*
- *Are sectoral regulators playing a role in incentivising critical infrastructure resilience?*
- *Are cost-benefit analysis used to prioritise resilience measures, evaluate their impact on costs of services, and find cost-sharing arrangements?*

Benchmark indicators

- *Implementation plans on critical infrastructure resilience*
- *Infrastructure regulations provisions on resilience*
- *Assessments of cost-benefits of resilience measures*

Examples of good practices

- *In Finland, the Energy Authority sets the requirements for business continuity and reliability standards in the electricity sector, and the National Emergency Supply Agency provides tools, guidance and methods for operators to comply with these regulations.*
- *In France, the State, CI operators and local authorities have agreed on measures to increase CI resilience for the risk of a major flood in Paris. This includes information-sharing, emergency preparedness and vulnerability reduction for existing and future infrastructure.*

6. Ensuring accountability and monitoring implementation of critical infrastructure resilience policies

Government should monitor implementation and evaluate progress in attaining resilience objectives, and define an accountability framework for critical infrastructure operators. Reviewing the effectiveness of the resilience policy tools should allow adjustments to a dynamic risk landscape and infrastructure innovations while taking into consideration the need for predictable and stable regulatory frameworks conducive to infrastructure investments.

Why is this important?

A comprehensive policy framework is a first step towards enhancing critical infrastructure resilience. Whether critical infrastructure will actually be resilient hinges on the implementation of the objectives and requirements put forward in these policies. Accountability mechanisms need to be set-up to ensure that operators carry out the stipulated resilience measures, such as criticality and vulnerability assessments, business continuity plans, back-up operating systems, exercises and stress tests, mutual aid agreements, retrofitting of assets, or risk financing mechanisms.

Monitoring implementation can take diverse forms including regular reporting, inspections and performance assessments or peer reviews. To strengthen accountability, fines for non-compliance, recognition/awards for the implementation of good practices and peer pressure through the use of open access evaluations/rankings are other available incentives that may motivate operators to prioritize investments in resilience measures. Regular evaluations are also useful to assess the effectiveness of policy instruments to strengthen critical infrastructure resilience and adapt them to keep up with the pace of innovations and emerging risk patterns.

Key policy questions:

- *Is there a regular monitoring of the implementation of resilience measures by critical infrastructure operators?*
- *Are there accountability frameworks in place to ensure that resilience measures are implemented?*
- *Are there reviews of the effectiveness of resilience policy instruments planned to adjust to a dynamic risk landscape?*
- *Are there joint exercises to test crisis and continuity management mechanisms?*

Benchmark indicators

- *Accountability frameworks for critical infrastructure stakeholders*
- *Revisions of critical infrastructure policies*

Examples of good practices

- *In Korea, the Ministry of Interior and Safety evaluates disaster response capacities of critical infrastructure operators every year, with a ranking that goes public. The peer pressure creates important incentives for operators to keep up their public image.*
- *10 years after its adoption, the European Commission is evaluating its Directive on European Critical Infrastructures to assess whether it remains relevant and effective.*

7. Addressing the transboundary dimension of infrastructure systems

Government should coordinate national critical infrastructure resilience policies with neighbouring countries and beyond, to address transboundary dependencies. International information-sharing mechanisms should be set up to assess risks and vulnerabilities across borders as well as to develop common approaches for critical infrastructure resilience.

Why is it important?

Interconnected and interdependent infrastructures cross borders bringing an important international dimension to resilience. Hazards and threats do not stop at national borders and integrated supply chains can propagate their consequences. In some cases, critical infrastructure provide services in multiple countries and different jurisdictions. This makes it more compelling to integrate international cooperation in critical infrastructure resilience policies. Sharing information and good practices, adopting common approaches, developing joint standards in critical infrastructure resilience are among the policy options that can foster international and transboundary cooperation in this area.

Key questions:

- *Are there international forums to foster exchange of good practices and to build common approaches for critical infrastructure resilience policies?*
- *Are there international information sharing platforms on risks and vulnerability for interdependent critical infrastructure?*
- *Are there cooperation mechanisms in place to define joint standards for critical infrastructure resilience with neighbouring countries?*

Benchmark indicators

- *International policy frameworks for critical infrastructure resilience*
- *Joint critical infrastructure resilience plans*

Examples of good practices

- *The Canada – United States Action Plan for Critical Infrastructure promotes an integrated approach to critical infrastructure protection and resilience by enhancing coordination of activities and facilitating continuous dialogue among cross-border stakeholders.*
- *The European Programme for Critical Infrastructure Protection (EPCIP) is a long-term programme that encompasses various instruments for the protection of critical infrastructure in the EU, including regular meetings of national CIP Points of Contact. Its external dimension includes regular meetings with strategic partners and was recently widened to include cooperation with neighbouring countries.*

References

G7 (2016), *G7 Ise-Shima Leaders' Declaration*, https://www.mofa.go.jp/files/000160266.pdf (accessed on 25 February 2019). [38]

OECD (2018), *Assessing Global Progress in the Governance of Critical Risks*, OECD Reviews of Risk Management Policies, OECD Publishing, Paris, https://dx.doi.org/10.1787/9789264309272-en. [2]

OECD (2017), *Getting Infrastructure Right: A framework for better governance*, OECD Publishing, Paris, https://dx.doi.org/10.1787/9789264272453-en. [11]

OECD (2014), *Boosting Resilience through Innovative Risk Governance*, OECD Reviews of Risk Management Policies, OECD Publishing, Paris, https://dx.doi.org/10.1787/9789264209114-en. [20]

OECD (2014), *Recommendation of the Council on the Governance of Critical Risks*, http://www.oecd.org/gov/risk/Critical-Risks-Recommendation.pdf (accessed on 25 February 2019). [1]

OECD and EU JRC (2018), *System thinking for critical infrastructure resilience and security - OECD/ JRC Workshop - OECD*, http://www.oecd.org/gov/risk/workshop-oecd-jrc-system-thinking-for-critical-infrastructure-resilience-and-security.htm (accessed on 25 February 2019). [41]

United Nations Office for Disaster Risk Reduction (2015), *Sendai Framework for Disaster Risk Reduction 2015 - 2030*, https://www.unisdr.org/files/43291_sendaiframeworkfordrren.pdf (accessed on 25 February 2019). [39]

ORGANISATION FOR ECONOMIC CO-OPERATION AND DEVELOPMENT

The OECD is a unique forum where governments work together to address the economic, social and environmental challenges of globalisation. The OECD is also at the forefront of efforts to understand and to help governments respond to new developments and concerns, such as corporate governance, the information economy and the challenges of an ageing population. The Organisation provides a setting where governments can compare policy experiences, seek answers to common problems, identify good practice and work to co-ordinate domestic and international policies.

The OECD member countries are: Australia, Austria, Belgium, Canada, Chile, the Czech Republic, Denmark, Estonia, Finland, France, Germany, Greece, Hungary, Iceland, Ireland, Israel, Italy, Japan, Korea, Latvia, Lithuania, Luxembourg, Mexico, the Netherlands, New Zealand, Norway, Poland, Portugal, the Slovak Republic, Slovenia, Spain, Sweden, Switzerland, Turkey, the United Kingdom and the United States. The European Union takes part in the work of the OECD.

OECD Publishing disseminates widely the results of the Organisation's statistics gathering and research on economic, social and environmental issues, as well as the conventions, guidelines and standards agreed by its members.

OECD PUBLISHING, 2, rue André-Pascal, 75775 PARIS CEDEX 16
ISBN 978-92-64-53346-2 – 2019

www.ingramcontent.com/pod-product-compliance
Lightning Source LLC
LaVergne TN
LVHW081410110826
845149LV00010B/1694

* 9 7 8 9 2 6 4 5 3 3 4 6 2 *